TRELLISES, PLANTERS & RAISED BEDS

50 Easy, Unique, and Useful Projects You Can Make with Common Tools and Materials

COOL
SPRINGS
PRESS

Growing Successful Gardeners™

MINNEAPOLIS, MINNESOTA

First published in 2013 by Cool Springs Press, an imprint of the Quarto Publishing Group USA Inc., 400 First Avenue North, Suite 400, Minneapolis, MN 55401

Cool Springs Press titles are also available at discounts in bulk quantity for industrial or sales-promotional use. For details write to Special Sales Manager at Quarto Publishing Group USA Inc., 400 North First Avenue, Suite 400, Minneapolis, MN 55401 USA. To find out more about our books, visit us online at www.coolspringspress.com.

Library of Congress Cataloging-in-Publication Data

Trellises, planters & raised beds : 50 easy, unique and useful garden projects you can make with simple tools & everyday items.
    p. cm.
  Includes index.
  ISBN 978-1-59186-545-2 (softcover)
  1. Trellises—Design and construction. 2. Plant containers—Design and construction.
  3. Beds (Gardens) I. Cool Springs Press. II. Title: Trellises, planters and raised beds.

  SB463.5.T74 2013
  681'.7631—dc23

              2012044655

Acquisitions Editor: Mark Johanson
Design Manager: Brad Springer
Design: Simon Larkin
Layout: Diana Boger
Illustrations: Greg Maxson
Photography: rau+barber, Isaiah King, Tracy Walsh, Joel Schnell, Christa Matthews
Project Designs: Eric Smith, Philip Schmidt, Dan Cary, Dawn King
Carpentry: Eric Smith
Technical Editor: Chris Marshall

Printed in China
10 9 8

Photo Credits:
Page 6: Adrian Sherratt/Alamy
Page 8: (top) iStockphoto.com; (bottom) Shutterstock.com
Page 9: (top) Shutterstock.com; (bottom) iStockphoto.com
Page 10: Shutterstock.com
Page 12: Shutterstock.com
Page 13: iStockphoto.com
Page 15: Adrian Sherratt/Alamy
Page 19 (bottom): Ottmar Bierwagen
Page 73: Shutterstock.com
Page 89 (bottom): Janet Johnson/Garden Picture Library/ Getty Images
Page 103: Shutterstock.com
Page 158: Tracy Walsh
Page 159 (both): Shutterstock.com
Page 161: Shutterstock.com
Page 164 (both): Shutterstock.com
Page 168 (bottom): Shutterstock.com

CONTENTS

45

146

154

93

114

62

143

74

42

90

158

84

87

110

161

165

25

INTRODUCTION

Looking for better ways to grow your garden? *Trellises, Planters & Raised Beds* has a whole bookful of them. In the following pages you'll find plans, ideas, inspirational photos, how-to instructions, and practical advice simple enough for a beginner to understand, but also varied and creative enough for experienced gardeners to find useful. You'll learn how to build time-tested designs for trellises, planters, and raised beds that look good and work well in any garden, but you'll also be exposed to the fertile imaginings of numerous gardeners and woodworkers who've found ways to transform standard, home-center materials into eye-catching garden structures that bring out the best in plants and flowers.

Getting started is easy, whether you're looking for a way to bring some green to a tiny porch or apartment terrace (check out Bamboo Bundle, page 90, or the Mini Planter on page 81), trying to start a small-scale vegetable farm to avoid the cost and plastic flavor of supermarket produce (see Lettuce Table, page 154, and Utility Raised Bed, page 158), or searching for something that your climbing plants can climb besides the house siding and each other (just about anything in the Trellises chapter will work). Most of the projects can be built with a saw, a drill, and basic hand tools, although a few don't need even that minimal tool kit, and can be put together with just a pair of hands and a shovel (Rock Garden, page 161; Raised Bed Kits, page 152). No matter what your skill level is, you'll find plenty of projects in this book that you can make, projects that will look great out in your garden or in your home—all with clear how-to photos and easy-to-follow instructions.

Trellises, Planters & Raised Beds is organized into three chapters, with each chapter having enough projects to select from that you won't have any trouble finding the right one for your garden. Some are shovel-ready—just pick up some materials at the home center and start building. Others require more prep time. For instance, stick trellises require that you collect suitable branches or saplings, and finding the right pallet for the pallet planter may require a few expeditions to your local warehouse district. A few of the projects are meant mostly for inspiration: grab a few ideas and then build your own version someday. But whether you're looking for step-by-step instructions, useful tips, and techniques, or just fodder for off-season daydreams, you'll find what you need inside.

GALLERY OF IDEAS

There are few limits on what you can do with your garden, as long as it keeps your plants happy and healthy. Pay attention to the basics—good soil, good drainage, plenty of sunlight and room to grow—and the plants will know what to do.

The project ideas on the next few pages show just a few of the many ways you can fill your home and yard with lush, vigorous plants without spending a fortune on materials and professional landscaping. You may have to wait for better weather to start planting, but you can start planning and building right now, and these designs will help get you started.

TOP: Raised beds make it easy to grow striking collections of plants.

ABOVE: Create densely planted, highly productive growing spaces on poor-quality soil.

ABOVE: This raised bed was constructed by dropping a dump-truck load of good soil on top of the existing sandy soil, shaping the soil with logs and old bricks and then planting with a mix of flowers, trees, and other plants that would have been doomed in the sand.

RIGHT: Veggies love the fertile, well-drained soil used in raised beds. Avoid using pressure-treated wood to build the frames if there's any chance you'll be planting edibles. Instead, use cedar or other naturally rot-resistant wood, or else line the inside of the treated wood with a rubber liner or other impermeable barrier that prevents chemicals in the wood from leaching into the soil.

This classic Zen garden combines a number of different elements, and has a backdrop of irregular raised beds formed by boulders and large stones.

A ladder, real or decorative, makes an interesting trellis for climbing plants. Rungs that can support a person easily support the heaviest fruits.

BELOW: Some planters are designed with very specific standards. The planters below are meant for use with the Square Foot Gardening approach popularized by garden writer Mel Bartholomew.

ABOVE: Turn weed trees into wattle fencing, then use it for raised beds. A rubber liner protects the wood and keeps the dirt in place, and cables tie the opposing sides together to keep them from bulging out under the weight of the dirt.

TRELLISES

Trellises are a great way to create dazzling displays of plants like climbing roses, honeysuckle, wisteria, sweet pea, clematis, and many others, giving them room to grow to their full potential and to soak in more sunshine than they might otherwise get in a crowded garden. But trellises also have very practical uses, both in backyard gardening and in commercial agriculture. For instance, trellises are essential for growing grapes, tomatoes, hops, raspberries, and other crops. Many garden vegetables—common plants like cucumbers, peas, beans, tomatoes, squash, and others—either need some type of trellis to climb or do better if they're trained to one, because they have fewer problems with rot, slugs, and other garden maladies associated with growing and ripening on the ground. Trellises also produce higher yields, because you can grow several square feet of produce on a square foot of ground.

Large trellises or trellises incorporated into fences are also an easy, inexpensive way to create privacy around your yard (and sometimes a nicer view) or to turn an exposed concrete patio into a pleasant outdoor room. Another good use: install a few trellises along the front of your house. You can increase your home's curb appeal by covering bare siding with rich green accents of ivy and the eye-capturing colors of climbing flowers.

To build a basic trellis all you need to do is fasten some horizontal pieces of wood or pipe or rope to vertical supports with nails, screws, or wire. The Sandwich Board Trellis on page 32 and the Bamboo Trellis on page 20 are good examples of classic garden trellises—they're simple to make, they get the job done, and when they start to decay several years down the road they're easy to replace. Despite their simplicity, they're also very attractive. And that's one of the pleasures of making trellises. As the projects in this chapter show, there are any number of ways to turn these basic, functional forms into works of garden art without compromising their purpose. The Frame Trellis on page 62 is a good example. Grab a handful of branches and fasten them together, and somehow they become very pleasing to look at. And with vines woven through them they'll look even better.

The most common materials used for trellises are rot-resistant wood, wire, metal pipes and twine or rope, but ordinary branches, and saplings make great trellises, too, and the material is free. Bamboo and copper pipe are also good materials to work with. Get creative. The Bamboo Trellis (page 20), the Frame Trellis (page 62), and the Copper Coil Trellis (page 42) are all good examples of how to make great designs with inexpensive, ordinary materials.

The best way to get started with your own trellis is to decide what you want to plant—small, light beans or peas, heavy tomatoes or melons, climbing flowers, or vines of ivy—and then pick a trellis from the designs in this chapter that suits the purpose. Or just use one as inspiration for your own great-looking trellis, tripod or obelisk.

CLASSIC GARDEN OBELISK

The obelisk is a simple form: four legs spread at the bottom and coming together at the top. The interpretation of the form seen here is relatively simple, although the angle cuts at the tops of the 2 x 2 legs might tax your geometry skills a bit. If that's true, no problem: just butt them all together and put a bigger finial on top.

People have been building obelisks and pyramids for thousands of years, using the natural beauty of the shape for everything from immense monuments to small toys—and garden trellises. Obelisks look impressive and complicated, but are actually simple to construct. They're just four equal posts joined at the top, but somehow they create a very attractive shape that looks perfect when overgrown with climbing plants and flowers.

The only tools you need to build this obelisk trellis are a saw, a drill, and a framing square. There's no complicated measuring, and just a little bit of tricky cutting involved.

TOOLS & MATERIALS

- 2 x 2" x 8 ft. pine (4)
- 1 x 2" x 8 ft. pine (3)
- Pine screen retainer molding mold x 10 ft. (2)
- Finial
- 2 and 2½" deck screws (1 lb.)
- 4d galvanized finish nails (8)
- Drill
- Countersink bit
- Drill bits
- Saw (hand, jigsaw or circular saw)
- Framing square

■ Customize Your Obelisk

The obelisk shown here will stand almost 5-ft. high, including the finial, and will measure 24 x 24" at the base. The finial at the top has a 2¾" diameter base, so the 2 x 2 posts each need to be 1" square at the top to provide a solid base and to have the end grain covered. The sides of the obelisk will slope 1 ft. outward for every 5 vertical ft. However, you can easily make the obelisk wider, narrower, taller, or shorter by revising the numbers from what we show in Illustration 1. Here's how it's done:

Divide the side of the obelisk into two right triangles. Half of our 24" base is 12" wide by 5-ft. tall, which means it slopes 12" for every 5 ft. (which is the same as saying 1" for every 5"). However, if you'd rather have a 3-ft. wide obelisk that's 6-ft. tall, that slope changes to 1½-ft. for every 6 ft., so change the measurements on the square to 1½" and 6". That's all there is to it.

CUTTING LIST

KEY	PART	DIMENSION	PCS.	MATERIAL
A	Leg	1½ x 1½ x 61"	4	Exterior-rated wood
B	Lower cross piece	1½ x ¾ x 22" *	4	
C	Upper cross piece	1½ x ¾ x 16" *	4	
		* Cut to size		

HOW TO BUILD A CLASSIC GARDEN OBELISK

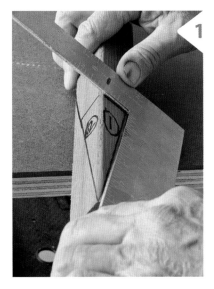

The first step is to mark the tops of the four legs for trimming. The general goal here is to trim each leg top so it has two beveled faces that meet in a point and then trim them to length. Use a framing square to mark a wedge shape on two adjoining faces at the top. The wedge should be 1" wide at a point 5" down from the leg top. Now, extend each of the four lines all the way to the edge of the workpiece, using a straightedge. You will have created two wedge shapes between 6 and 7" long. The wedges are the waste material you'll need to cut off.

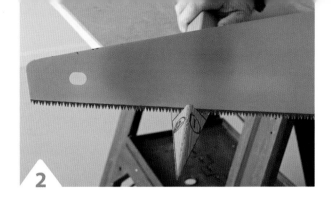

2

Using a handsaw, cut off one of the wedges. This will create a wedge-shaped waste piece. Then, flip your workpiece a quarter turn and cut off the other wedge. This waste piece won't be a complete wedge since some of the wood is already gone. What you'll be left with is a 2 x 2 that has two beveled faces meeting in a point. To finish the trimming of the leg tops, simply make a crosscut that follows the two 1" cutting lines you drew in the first step. This will leave a top that is 1" by 1" and is angled so it will be level when the legs are spread out. Make the other tops the same way. When you're done the four legs will fit together to form a flat 2 x 2" top with the leg bottoms 24" apart.

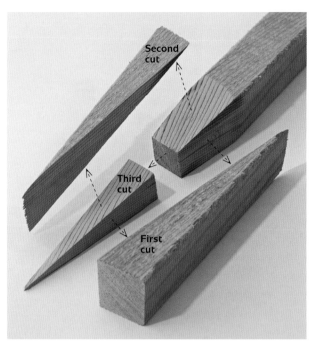

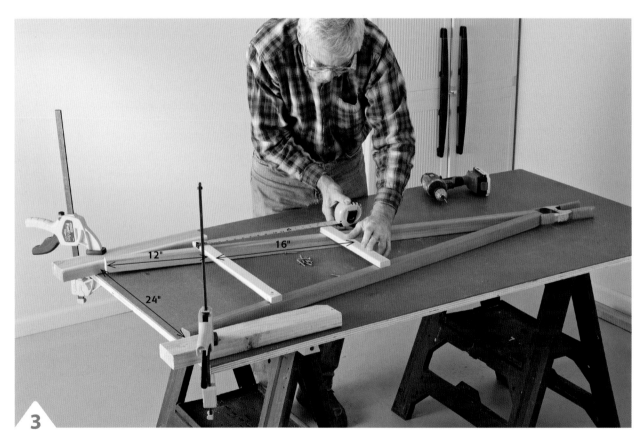

3

Space an obelisk leg pair 24" apart from outside to outside at the bottom and clamp them or wedge them between two pieces of wood spaced 24" apart. Clamp the beveled top ends together—the legs should naturally be close to 24". Cut a 1 x 2 to 22" long, lay it across the legs at 12" from the bottom, then mark and cut the 1 x 2 flush with the legs. Fasten with 2" screws driven through pilot holes. Cut and fasten another crosspiece 16" above the lower crosspiece (center to center). Join the tops of the 2 x 2 legs with a 2½" screw. Drill pilot holes for the screw to avoid splitting the ends. Remove the assembled leg pair and repeat the process with the other two obelisk legs.

4 Stand the two assembled leg pairs upright with the tops joined together. Clamp them and space the legs 24" apart. Mark two more sets of crosspieces, this time cutting them flush with the 1 x 2s, and fasten them to the 2 x 2s that are already installed, using screws driven through pilot holes. Then screw the four tops together. (Note: if you would like the 1 x 2s to match up perfectly at the corners, make compound miter cuts on the ends: Trace the leg on a horizontal 1 x 2, then draw a 45° line from both the top and bottom of the line, connect them on the face of the 1 x 2, and cut that angle.)

As an option, you can add diagonal crosspieces on the sides in an X pattern. Use screen retainer molding. Hold pieces of the molding in position and mark cutting lines directly on the molding. Cut it to fit with a handsaw. Attach it in an X pattern with 4d galvanized finish nails.

The final step is attaching the finial. If you're using a standard finial from a home center, just drill a hole for the integral lag screw in the center of the top and thread it in. If your finial does not come with an integral screw, nail and glue the finial to the tops of the posts. Apply a finish as desired. We painted this one a cheerful red tone with exterior latex semi-gloss.

This basic obelisk design is very adaptable to flowers or vegetables in any garden setting, big or small. It looks great painted in a fun color like the purple seen here or the red on page 16.

■ Tip

To install your obelisk in the garden or yard, position the completed project wherever you would like it to go and push the legs into the dirt to level it. If you're concerned that the obelisk might get blown or pushed over, hammer in 12" lengths of rebar, conduit or other staking material next to one or two legs and tie them tightly to the legs with galvanized wire.

BAMBOO TRELLIS

A bamboo trellis can be fashioned in just about any size or configuration for whichever climbing plant you wish. You can build a taller version for pole beans and other aggressive climbers, add more crosspieces, or weave string between poles to support delicate vines.

Bamboo is an ideal material for building garden trellises and other structures to support climbing plants in your garden. Bamboo poles are lightweight, strong, and naturally decay-resistant. And because bamboo is really a giant grass, it looks right at home in any garden setting. It is also a completely renewable resource.

In this easy project, you'll learn the traditional technique for building with natural bamboo poles and lashing twine. The trellis shown is freestanding and is held upright with rebar rods (used for concrete reinforcement) driven into the ground. You can apply the same techniques to create your own trellis designs, tailoring the height, length, and pole spacing to suit your plants and planting area.

Bamboo poles are sold through online retailers, local bamboo suppliers (where available), import stores, and some garden centers. The poles come in sizes ranging from about ¼" to 5" in diameter and in lengths up to 20 ft. or so. Of course, the diameters are approximate and variable, since this is a natural product. In this project as shown, the vertical supports are 1½" in diameter and the horizontal and vertical crosspieces are 1" in diameter.

While bamboo can survive many years of exposure to the elements, a bamboo trellis is lightweight enough that you can simply pull it off of its supports and store it over winter—a good idea in colder climates. Ground contact or burial of bamboo poles does lead to premature rot, so prop up the trellis poles on stones or brick to prevent ground contact. A small pile of stones hides the rebar and creates an attractive base around each support pole.

TOOLS & MATERIALS

- Tape measure
- Hacksaw
- Hammer
- Scissors
- Hand maul

- 5-ft. 1½"-dia. bamboo poles (3)
- 5-ft. 1"-dia. bamboo poles (2)
- 4-ft. 1"-dia. bamboo poles (4)
- 2-ft. length of #2 rebar or metal rod (1)
- 3-ft. lengths of #3 rebar (3)

- Level
- Stones
- Waxed lashing twine
- Eye and ear protection
- Work gloves

HOW TO BUILD A BAMBOO TRELLIS

1 Trim off the top end of each vertical bamboo pole just above a node (the rings on the pole), using a hacksaw or any other saw with very fine teeth. The solid membrane of the node will serve as a cap to prevent water from collecting inside the pole. Trim the three 1½"-dia. vertical support poles and four 1"-dia. vertical crosspieces.

2 Measuring from the trimmed top ends of the vertical poles, cut the two outer support poles to length at 48", and cut the four vertical crosspieces at 36". The middle support pole and horizontal crosspieces should be about 60" long; cut them to length only if necessary.

Break through the nodes in the bottoms of the three vertical support poles to create clear passage for the rebar stakes. Do this by using a hammer and #2 rebar or other metal rod. Clear any nodes within the bottom 18" of each pole. Tip: If the first node is close to the end, drill several holes through the node before breaking it out to help prevent the pole from splitting.

3

LASHING TECHNIQUE

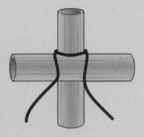

1 Fold a 4-ft.-long piece of waxed twine in half and wrap it around the bottom cane.

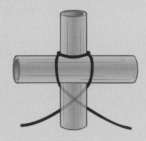

2 Pull both ends of the twine across the top cane and cross them underneath the bottom cane.

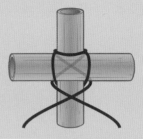

3 Pull the twine ends back up and cross them over the top cane.

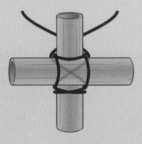

4 Cross the twine underneath the joint, forming an X.

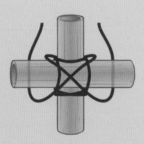

5 Lift the ends up and make an X across the top of the joint.

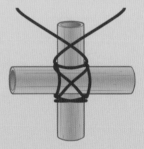

6 Wrap the bottom cane from below and then across the top, next to the joint.

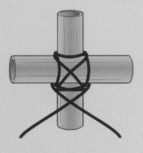

7 Wrap the bottom cane on the other side of the joint.

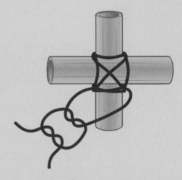

8 Tie a square knot and then trim off the twine ends.

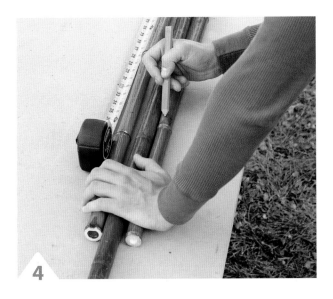

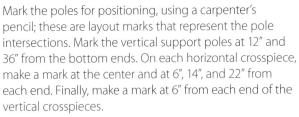

4

Mark the poles for positioning, using a carpenter's pencil; these are layout marks that represent the pole intersections. Mark the vertical support poles at 12" and 36" from the bottom ends. On each horizontal crosspiece, make a mark at the center and at 6", 14", and 22" from each end. Finally, make a mark at 6" from each end of the vertical crosspieces.

5

Lay out the poles on a flat work surface, starting with the vertical support poles. Let the bottom ends of the poles overhang the edge of the work surface beyond the lower layout marks so you can get at them more easily. Position the bottom horizontal crosspiece on top of the support poles using the layout marks for positioning.

6

Lash the crosspiece to each support pole, using a 60"-long piece of waxed lashing twine; see Lashing Technique, previous page. When each lashing is complete, trim the excess twine with scissors.

7

Lash the remaining horizontal crosspiece at the upper marks on the support poles. Position the vertical crosspieces on top of the horizontals, and lash the poles together at each intersection.

8 Position the completed trellis framework in the desired location of the garden or planting bed. The back sides of the vertical support poles should face away from the planting area. Press down on the framework so the vertical support poles make an impression in the soil, marking the locations of the rebar stakes.

9 Drive a 36" length of #3 rebar (or other size that fits snugly inside the vertical support poles) into the soil at each pole impression, using a hand maul. Use a level to check the bar for plumb as you work. Drive the bars 18" into the soil.

10 Set stones, bricks, or other bits of masonry material around each piece of rebar. Fit the ends of the vertical support poles over the rebar so they stand squarely on the stones. Check the trellis with a level and adjust for square or plumb, as needed, by adding or moving the stones.

■ Rebar

Rebar (sometimes called "re-rod") is a metal rod that is placed in a concrete form before the concrete is poured to reinforce the concrete when it hardens. There are many ways to use it around the house and yard that do not involve concrete at all, as it is a very hard, durable and inexpensive material. You will see rebar described as #3 or #4—these numbers are actually the numerator in the fraction describing the diameter of the rebar, with "8" as the denominator. Thus a #3 rebar has a diameter of ⅜". Rebar is difficult to cut. Don't even bother going at it with a hacksaw. The best tool is a metal cutoff saw, but if you don't have access to one you can install a bi-metal blade in a reciprocating saw. Another option is to use an abrasive cutting wheel in a hand-held angle grinder.

TRIPOD TRELLIS

A simple tripod or teepee-style trellis is a classic garden helper. It couldn't be easier to install, and it folds up into a compact unit for off-season storage. This design uses 2 x 2 lumber for its three legs. Each gets a tapered bottom end for pushing into the soil to anchor the trellis.

The tops of the legs are joined with a clever system using some basic hardware. Each leg is fitted with an eye lag. When it's time to install the trellis, you capture the eyes with a quick link, which is a chain link that opens and closes with its own coupling nut. Both eye lags and quick links are commonly available at hardware stores and home centers. Look for eye lags in the general hardware section and for quick links among the chain and rope. Be sure to confirm that the quick link opens far enough to accommodate the eye part of the lag—if in doubt, buy the larger size. This sturdy trellis is perfect for supporting pole beans and other tall climbers.

Practically as portable as a camera tripod, this garden trellis sets up anywhere it is needed. You can't adjust the height, but it is extremely sturdy.

HOW TO BUILD A TRIPOD TRELLIS

TOOLS & MATERIALS

- ☐ 8-ft. rot-resistant 2 x 2s, cut to 72" (3)
- ☐ ¼" x 2½" galvanized or stainless steel eye lags (3)
- ☐ Galvanized or stainless steel quick link (locking chain link)
- ☐ 1¼" deck screws (1 lb.)
- ☐ Jute or hemp twine
- ☐ Tape measure
- ☐ Saw
- ☐ Speed square
- ☐ Sandpaper
- ☐ Drill
- ☐ ³⁄₁₆" bit
- ☐ Hammer
- ☐ Screwdriver
- ☐ Scissors

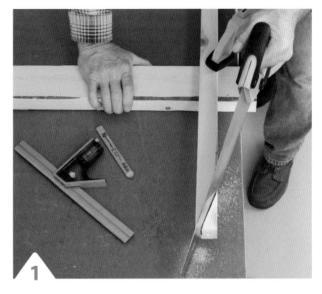

To build the trellis, first cut the 2 x 2 legs 72" long, then taper the ends. To mark the taper cutting lines, draw a line across one face of each leg, 3" from the bottom end. On one of the adjacent faces of the board, mark ¼" from the bottom side. Connect the line and the mark to create a diagonal cutting line for tapering the leg end. Cut the tapers with a jigsaw or handsaw.

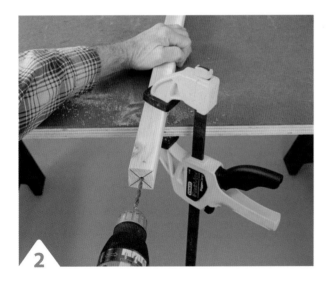

Mark the centers of the tops of the three legs, then drill pilot holes for the eye lags. The holes should be about 2" deep. Use a bit just a little smaller than the threads on the eye lag. If the hole is too small the wood may split as you turn the screw in. For the ¼" dia. eye lags seen here, a ³⁄₁₆" pilot hole is drilled.

Tip: You can locate the precise center of the board end by drawing diagonal lines from corner to corner.

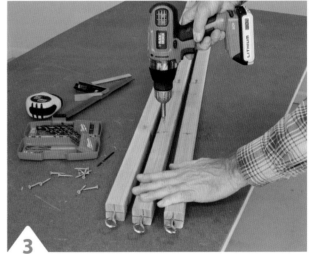

Next, lay the three poles side by side and mark the cord rung locations on each of them. Place the marks 12" apart, measuring down from the top. Predrill and drive 1¼" screws at each mark, leaving the screws about ⅜" out so the twine can be wrapped around them. The screws should all go on the long side of the leg (the side with the taper).

Connect the legs at their top ends by fitting the eye lags onto a single quick link. Try to keep the legs turned so the screws face outward. This may take a little fussing if the quick link is on the small side—turning the bolts a quarter turn in or out will help.

Once the legs are all connected, spread them apart so they're roughly equidistant and spaced 3 to 5 ft. apart. Push the tapers several inches into the ground so the trellis is stable. Then start wrapping the twine around the legs. Tie one end of the twine to the bottom screw on one of the legs; you'll tie off all of the twine to this same leg, so choose the least visible leg. Run the twine across to the next leg and wrap it once around the bottom screw, keeping the twine as taut as possible. Do the same at the third leg, then tie off the twine on the first leg. Tie the remaining rungs in the same fashion to complete the trellis.

Set your tripod up in your garden. At the end of the growing season, just pull the legs out, collapse the tripod and store it away until spring. Replace the twine every year or two, as needed.

COPPER LADDER
TRELLIS

This stately trellis is a beautiful example of how to successfully blend building materials in your yard or garden. In this case, copper tubing and cedar mesh together very effectively.

Copper and cedar make a great combination. This trellis combines them in a simple and refined design. It's a design that will look at home in just about any garden. As this trellis ages the wood and copper will both change colors and gain a warm, weathered patina. The only tools you need to build this trellis are a jigsaw, a drill/driver, a square, and a pipe cutter (a plumbing tool that is available in the plumbing department of any hardware store for less than $10). Once you have all the materials on hand, you can construct this trellis and have it set in the ground in half a day.

TOOLS & MATERIALS

- 2 x 4" x 8-ft. rot-resistant wood (2)
- 1 x 8" x 8-ft. rot-resistant wood (2)
- ½" x 10-ft. copper pipe (2)
- 2" deck screws (1 lb.)
- 100- or 120-grit sandpaper
- Non-compactable gravel

- Drill
- ⅝" drill bit
- Saw
- Pipe cutter
- Jigsaw
- Compass

- Masking tape
- Posthole digger
- Level
- Shovel

CUTTING LIST

KEY	PART	DIMENSION	PCS.	MATERIAL
A	Posts	1½ x 3 ½" x 8 ft.	2	Cedar
B	Top rails	¾ x 7¼ x 48"	2	Cedar
C	Bottom rails	¾ x 7¼ x 36"	2	Cedar
D	Copper tubes	½ x 30"	8	Copper pipe

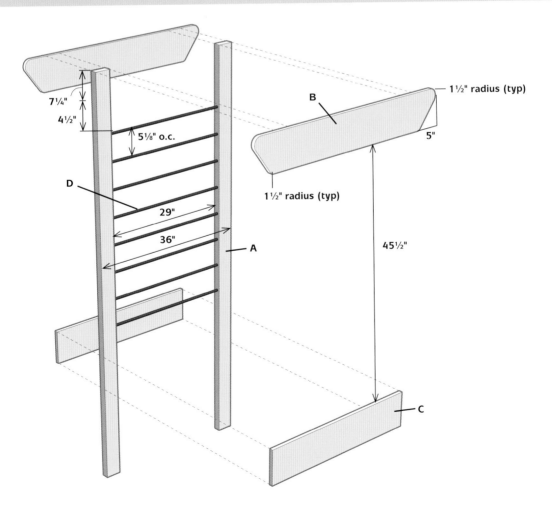

HOW TO MAKE A COPPER LADDER TRELLIS

The posts have a series of equally-spaced holes that contain the copper tubing. The holes must be drilled in the same positions on both posts to keep the tubing in alignment. Place the posts upright on their narrow edges and next to each other with their ends flush. Clamp the posts together to keep them from moving as you mark the hole locations. Starting from the top, mark off 7¼" to mark bottom of top rail, then 4½" to the top of the first copper pipe and then 5⅛" from center

to center for the rest. The bottom rail is 45½" from the top rail (52¾" from the top of the post). Mark the holes across both posts using a speed square, then mark the center of each post on the lines. Next, bore a ⅝" dia. x ¾"-deep hole at each mark, keeping the drill as straight as possible as you drill into the wood. Place tape on the drill bit to mark the ¾" drilling depth, and watch it carefully as you drill. Sand off the hole alignment marks after all of the holes are bored.

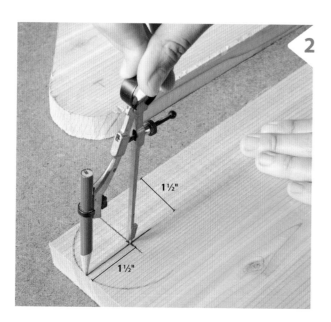

Cut the top and bottom rail parts to length. Create the profiles for the ends of the top rails using a pencil, compass, and straight edge. The top curve is a 1½" radius. Set the compass leg at 1½" from the top of the board and 1½" from the end of the board. The bottom curve is a 1" radius with the compass leg set at 1" up from the bottom and 5" in from the end of the board. After the curves are traced with the compass, draw a line between the furthest outside edge of each curve to connect them. Cut the lines with a jigsaw. Use a scrolling bit if possible so you can cut the curved ends smoothly. Finally, sand the sawblade marks and rough edges smooth. Before assembling the trellis, apply an exterior-rated finish or leave the wood unfinished to weather naturally.

3 Cut the ½"-dia. copper tubing into eight 30" long pieces using the pipe cutter. Don't use a jigsaw for this step—it will leave jagged edges that will be difficult or impossible to fit into the ⅝" holes. Place the ends of the copper tubing pieces in all the holes in one of the posts. Angle the other post just enough so that you can set the pipes in the holes one at a time—don't try to do them all at once.

4 Space the posts 29" apart so that the 36" bottom rails come to the edge of the posts. Mark the lower rail location. Attach the top and bottom rails with pre-drilled 2" deck screws. If any of the copper falls out, which might happen if one of the holes was drilled too deep, just squeeze some caulk or construction glue into the hole and slide the pipe in ½". The final step is to place the trellis in your garden. Dig two 6"-dia. x 24"-deep holes for the posts. Space the center of the holes 32½" apart. Pour several inches of non-compactable gravel in the bottom of the holes to allow water to drain away from the post. Place the posts in the holes and have a helper hold them plumb and level as you fill around the posts with more gravel. Now all that's left to do is plant a climbing-type plant and wait for it to cover the trellis.

SANDWICH BOARD TRELLIS

A sandwich board trellis is made with two identical frames held together with simple hinges. The pointed feet in this design keep the main frame parts off the ground (to forestall decay) and dig into the soil for added stability.

Inspired by the ingeniously simple and stable structure of a sidewalk sandwich board sign, the A-frame trellis has, in one form or another, proved a trusty workhorse for many home gardeners. Its basic design offers several advantages. It's portable, so you can move it between beds and quickly set it up wherever plants need support, as well as store it away for winter. And, like a sidewalk sign, the trellis is hinged at the top, allowing you to spread the two frames any distance apart you need to fit a bed or accommodate plant growth.

This trellis design is incredibly easy to build and just as easy to customize. Simply change the lengths of the frame pieces to make your trellis taller or shorter, wider or narrower. The other optional feature is the material used for the webbing within the frames. In the photo on this page, jute twine is threaded through holes in the frame to create a roughly

6½" square grid for supporting climbing plants. What's nice about the twine is that you can snip it off at the end of the season and compost it with the old vines—there's none of that tedious work of picking off the dried tendrils from the webbing. Other popular webbing materials that you can use on this trellis are chicken wire and yard fencing (see page 37).

All of the trellis frame parts are made with 1 × 4 cedar boards (or other naturally decay-resistant wood). These can be rough or smooth and don't need to be high-grade. You can even use unstained fence planks, which come in 6-ft. lengths and tend to be cheaper than 1 × 4 dimension lumber.

TOOLS & MATERIALS

- **Tape measure**
- **Circular saw**
- **Framing square**
- **Clamps**
- **Drill and bits**
- **Scissors**
- **Marker**

- **8-ft. cedar 1 × 4 (6)**
- **Deck screws, 1¼" (32) and 2" (12)**
- **3"-long galvanized or stainless steel butt hinges with screws (2)**
- **Heavy jute or hemp twine (250 ft.)**
- **Eye and ear protection**
- **Work gloves**

HOW TO BUILD A SANDWICH BOARD TRELLIS

Cut the frame parts to length from 1 × 4 lumber, using a circular saw or power miter saw. To make the 6-ft. version seen here, cut four stiles (the side pieces) at 72", and cut four rails (the top and bottom pieces) at 48".

Test-fit the parts of one frame to make sure it all works properly. Then, set the stiles facedown on your work surface so they're about 48" apart. Set a rail (the horizontal board) across both stiles at the top and bottom ends of the stiles. Make sure the rail ends are flush with the ends and outside edges of the stiles. Check one of the corners with a framing square, and clamp the rail to the stile at that corner.

3

4

With the parts still lined up and held together securely, drill pilot holes through the rail and into the stile. Fasten the rail to the stile with four 1¼" deck screws. Repeat the clamping, squaring, fastening process at each corner to complete the frame. Assemble the other frame in the same manner.

Cut the four pointed feet to length at 12" each, using cut-off scraps of wood. At one end of each foot piece, mark the center of the board's width (about 1¾" from the side edges). Then, mark each side edge at 2" from the same end of the foot. Draw a line between the side marks and center mark. Cut along these lines to create the pointed end for each foot. Be sure to clamp the work piece securely. You can use a handsaw or jigsaw instead of the circular saw shown here if it is more comfortable.

5

Install each foot at the bottom corner of a frame so its top (square) end is flush with the top edge of the rail, and its side edge is flush with the end of the rail. Fasten the foot to the rail and stile with two or three 2" screws (drill pilot holes first); make sure these are offset from the original screws fastening the rails to the stiles.

Mark the hole locations for the twine, 1" from the inside edge of each frame member. Mark the outer holes on each piece about 1" from the adjacent rails/stiles, then space the remaining holes at about 6½" intervals in between. Drill holes that are slightly larger than the thickness of the twine.

Attach an exterior-rated butt hinge to the top rail on each frame. Position one hinge 5" from each side edge on one of the frames. Drill pilot holes and fasten the hinge with the screws that came with the hinge. Fasten the other half of each hinge to the other frame, making sure the gap between the rails is even.

Thread the horizontal strings first. Start by cutting 22 lengths of twine at about 60" long. Feed one end of each string through the front of a stile hole and knot it in back. Pull the string straight across to the other stile, down through the corresponding hole, and tie it with a double knot so the string is taut.

Tie off each vertical string at the top rail, using a knot behind, as before (you'll need 14 strings at about 96" each). Pull each string taut and hold or clamp it in place over the corresponding hole in the bottom rail, then mark each horizontal string at the point where it intersects with the vertical string, using a marker. The marks will help you keep the grid in line as you install the vertical strings.

Run the vertical strings from top to bottom, wrapping once around each horizontal string at the marked intersection. Keep the string taut as you work, and tie off the string at the bottom rail with a double knot, as before. Complete the webbing for the other frame, following the same process. For other webbing options, see the next page.

CEDAR TONES

It takes just a few weeks in the garden for cedar boards to take on a soft gray tone that gives it a slightly weathered appearance. Note how the 6 x 6" grid of the jute webbing is perfectly spaced for a climbing squash plant.

VARIATIONS

You can substitute chicken wire (technically, this is called poultry netting) for the twine if you want to create permanent webbing. Cut each wire panel to size (46 × 70" as seen here) using wire cutters or aviation snips. Center the panel over the front face of the frame and secure it with galvanized staples along one stile. Pull the panel taut and staple it along the other stile, then along the top and bottom rails.

Vinyl-coated wire fencing on a short frame makes a great trellis for melons, tomatoes, and other sprawling varieties that bear heavier fruit. Cut the fencing about 2" shorter and narrower than the outsides of the trellis frames, and fasten it to the outside faces with galvanized heavy-duty staples or poultry staples (U-shaped nails).

ROLL-UP CRITTER FENCE

Protect plants that the local fauna find delicious with a critter cage like this. It can be set up when your plants are vulnerable to rabbits and other small creatures, and then removed and stored easily when it is no longer needed.

Every gardener has experienced the vexation and heartbreak of nurturing a plant week after week, watching it develop and mature, leaving fruit on the vine until just the right moment . . . only to walk out one morning to discover their prized tomato lying squashed on the ground, half-eaten by a squirrel or rabbit.

Of course, the best way to avoid this sad fate is by covering your plants with some kind of enclosure, but fencing can be a pain to set up, and draping bird netting over plants is a daily exercise in frustration. Not so with this handy, reusable critter fence. The fencing is galvanized wire mesh, a grid of heavy-duty wire that stands up well on its own yet is easy to bend to any desired shape. Pointed 2 x 2 posts add rigidity to the mesh and anchor the enclosure firmly for the entire season.

But perhaps the best feature of this critter guard is its door. To access your plant for tending and harvesting, just undo the two hook-and-eye latches and swing open the hinged door (the door post isn't staked down); there's no fussing with droopy netting or wrestling with springy wire. When the growing season's over, simply pull up the fence and posts (they're all attached) and roll up the fence to about half its installed size for compact storage.

TOOLS & MATERIALS

- 16-gauge galvanized wire mesh (10 ft.)
- 2 x 2" x 8-ft. pressure-treated wood (2); calculate quantity and length based on fencing height and length
- Galvanized staples (U-nails) (1 lb.)
- Galvanized or zinc hook-and-eye latches (2)

- Tape measure
- Permanent marker
- Leather work gloves
- Drill and $\frac{1}{16}$" bit
- Needlenose pliers

- Standard pliers
- Circular saw
- Wire cutters
- Clamps
- Hammer

■ How Much Fencing Do You Need?

Calculate the total length of fencing you need using the desired size of the completed enclosure and applying a bit of simple math. As an example, if you'd like to have a 3-ft.-dia. enclosure around your plant, multiply 36" x 3.1416 (the rounded value of pi):

36 x 3.1416 = 113.1

Round up your sum to the nearest whole number, then add 2" to find the total length of fence required. Therefore a 36"-dia. enclosure needs 116" of fencing. For a couple more examples, a 2-ft.-dia. enclosure needs 78" of fencing; a 4-ft. enclosure calls for 153" of fencing.

WEAR YOUR GLOVES!

CAUTION: Always wear heavy gloves when working with wire mesh. Cut wire ends can be very sharp, and the rolled-up fencing has a nasty way of springing up at you when you least expect it.

SMALL ANIMAL FENCING

The wire mesh used for the project as shown is half small grid to keep out critters like chipmunks, mice, and smaller varmints, and half larger grid for keeping out squirrels, rabbits, and larger animals. To prevent birds from entering from above, lay a round piece of mesh on top of the enclosure; there's no need to secure this, and you can simply pull it off whenever you need to access the plant. Just make sure to bend over or file any sharp wire ends from the top piece.

Flatten the fencing as well as you can by standing on the mesh and pulling it up from the floor ahead of your feet, gently taking out the bend. Flattening the wire makes it easier and safer to work with; it doesn't have to be perfect. For the best results, unroll the mesh with the concave side facing down, and stand on or weigh down the mesh to keep it flat to the floor as you work on it.

Typical small animal fencing is 28" wide, so this cage is 28" tall. You can buy wider fencing for a taller cage, but it won't have the graduated grid feature.

HOW TO MAKE A ROLL-UP CRITTER FENCE

Roll the fencing out, then measure and cut the length of wire fencing you need, using aviation snips. Cut off a 2-ft. section at one end for the door, leaving a flush-cut edge on both sides of the door. Cut the horizontal tails off one edge of the main section, but leave the tails on where the door was cut off so you can form hinges with them.

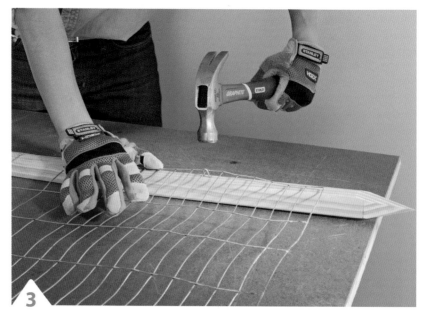

Cut the posts to length (which should be 6" longer than the height of the fencing you're using), then "sharpen" one end of each post by making bevel cuts on all four sides. The bevels will make it easier to pound the posts into the ground. Note that the non-hinge post for the door is cut short so it will not reach the ground and can swing freely.

Roll the fence backwards to take out some of the bend, then slide the fixed posts under the fence. Arrange them roughly equally across the length of the fencing. For a 2- or 3-ft.-dia. enclosure, plan to have one post at each end of the main fencing section (not including the door) and two posts in between; for a 4-ft. enclosure, use three posts in between. Fasten the mesh to the post with ¾" staple nails, starting with the post at the end that has no free wires.

The tops of the posts should be flush with the top edge of the fencing. Position the post at the starting edge of the fencing (the edge without the horizontal tails) so that the post extends about ¼" beyond the mesh. To install the last post before the door, position the post inside of the last vertical wire so the horizontal tails extend fully beyond the post. Fasten the post with staples, as with the others.

Install the door post flush with the top and bottom of the door and extending about ¼" past the end of the mesh. To attach the door to the main fence, use needlenose pliers to bend each tail of wire at the last post into a small U shape. Hook the vertical wire of the door mesh onto the U ends just below the horizontal mesh of the door. Close the U hooks with the pliers to create enclosed hinges. Position the fence upright and wrap it into a circular shape so the door post and first fixed post meet, with their top ends aligned and their outside faces flush with each other. Clamp the posts together and install two hook-and-eye latches for securing the door to the fixed post.

■ Using Your Critter Cage

Position the completed fence around your plant in the garden and close and latch the door. Fine-tune the shape of the mesh, bending the wire gently, as needed. When all looks good, carefully push or hammer the fixed posts into the soil, driving them in a little at a time to keep the top of the fence relatively level as you work. Stop when the bottom of the fencing touches the ground. Test the door operation and adjust the height of the mating fixed post, if necessary, so the door swings freely.

COPPER COIL TRELLIS

Absolutely elegant, this steeple-shaped trellis is fashioned from ordinary copper tubing and copper wire.

Trellises for supporting seasonal climbing plants are often utilitarian and makeshift. And that's fine. They do their job, and when the growing season's over, they get hauled into the shed or maybe they're scrapped and rebuilt again the next year.

This trellis is different. Made almost entirely of copper materials, it's designed for permanent installation (although moving it is no problem), and it looks good enough to be the star of the show even when it's supporting a tangle of eager young vines. In the off-season, the trellis becomes an appealing garden folly and makes an ideal structure for hanging twinkle lights for a wintertime or holiday decoration. Because it's made entirely from copper, it will last a lifetime.

The three trellis supports are rigid copper plumbing pipe, and the coil is ¼" flexible copper tubing, commonly used for water supply lines for refrigerator ice makers. All of the materials are available at any large home center. Choose your rigid pipes based on the size of your trellis and the weight of the plants it will support. Copper pipe comes in three types: K, M, and L. Type K has the thickest wall and is therefore the most expensive, while L is the standard type most commonly used for household water supply piping. For most applications, ½" type L pipe is suitable. It's also the cheapest option.

TOOLS & MATERIALS

- ½" x 10 ft. rigid copper pipe (2)
- ½" copper pipe caps (3)
- 20-ft. coil of ¼" flexible copper tubing
- Emery cloth or sandpaper
- ⅛" metal cutting bit
- #14 copper wire

- Pipe cutter
- Drill
- Tin snips
- Wire cutters
- Pliers
- Spring clamps

■ Flexible Copper Tubing

Flexible copper tubing is used mostly for water supply lines, as with an icemaker. It comes in 20 and 50 ft. rolls and in two or three thicknesses. For this project, ¼" dia. flexible tubing is adequate.

HOW TO MAKE A COPPER COIL TRELLIS

Cut the copper pipe into 5-ft. lengths (or other size) with a pipe cutter. Tap a drywall screw against the copper about 1" down from the top to make a dimple for a drill bit to catch on, then drill a ⅛" hole through both sides of each pipe. Slide a copper tube cap onto the top end of each pipe—a friction fit (as opposed to soldering) should be enough to hold the caps in place. Thread #14 copper wire (solid, not braided) through the holes, but cut it several inches long and join the ends with a single twist.

Set the bottoms of the three pipes far enough apart to create the size you want, spacing them equidistantly. Push the pipe ends into the ground (or tape them to the floor if you're working indoors). Adjust the pipes as needed until the three capped ends look symmetrical, then pull the wire tight and twist the ends. Leave just enough of a gap between the three pipes for the tubing to push through. Trim the excess wire and bend it flat.

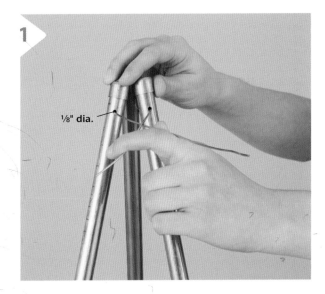

⅛" dia.

Place a 20 ft. coil of ¼" copper tubing over the top of the trellis assembly. Feed the end of the tubing from the center of the coil up through the gap between the three pipes so about 16" extends beyond the top of the collar; you'll use this to make a decorative finial shape at the top of the trellis. Tie the tubing to one of the three pipes using copper wire. Twist and tighten the wire with pliers. Trim the excess wire and bend over the cut ends. Gently push the coil of tubing downward while spiraling it around the three pipes. Bend the tubing as needed to create a smooth spiral that stays in contact with all three pipes. Clamp the tubing with spring clamps every turn or two to hold it in place as you unroll it.

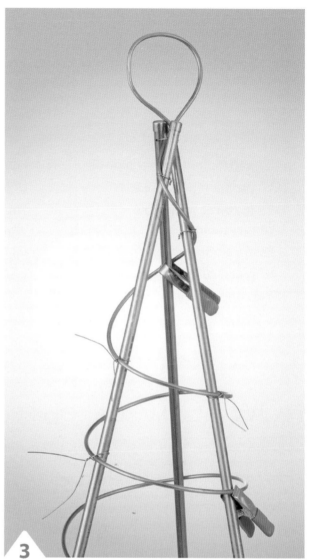

2

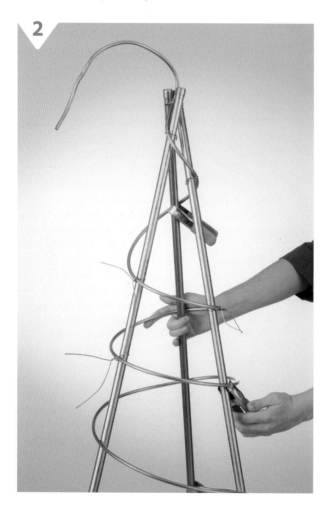

3

Once the spiral looks good, tie the tubing to the pipes with the copper wire, working your way down from the top of the trellis. Tighten the wire with pliers, nip off the excess, and bend over the cut ends. Finally, shape the top end of the tubing into a decorative form, as desired, then tie off the free end to the tubing itself or to one of the pipes. If you haven't already done so, set it in the garden and push the legs down into the soil.

DIAMOND TRELLIS

The primary purpose of a trellis is to support climbing plants such as clematis or morning glory. But a trellis also serves as a visually pleasing vertical design element that can offer additional benefits, including blocking sun and wind. Paired with a pergola overhead structure, a trellis can provide a living screen to create an intimate nook in the landscape. Or, when placed against a wall, a trellis can add a cottage feel to your home while allowing plantlife to scale its wooden rungs and lend its green character to your space.

This diamond trellis is intensely decorative and is truly eye candy for any garden or yard. But it is also functional, and it will work to support

(continued next page)

A well-designed trellis supports climbing plants during the growing season, and it also contributes to the appearance of the yard during the offseason when the plants die back.

your plants within any space that you put it. Because it is so adaptable, think hard before deciding whether you want to build it exactly as shown. What is the purpose for this trellis? What are the growing habits of the vines that will climb the structure? Fast growers, for example, require either a taller trellis or constant pruning. Also consider what, if anything, you are trying to cover up with a trellis. Perhaps it is a utility area with garbage cans or recycling bins; maybe it is a compost area; or, it might even be an unsightly view that is not part of your property.

You can experiment with the trellis motif—how cedar pieces are arranged in patterns to form the wall. This one was built with diamonds, but you can switch shapes to mimic existing themes in your garden.

CUTTING LIST

KEY	PART	PIECES	DIMENSION
A	Base Rail	2	¾ × 1½ × 40"
B	Upright-outer	2	¾ × 1½ × 91"
C	Upright-inner	2	¾ × 1½ × 93"
D	Upright-center	1	¾ × 1½ × 89"
E	Rail	6	¾ × 1½ × 38"
F	Filler-long	2	¾ × 1½ × 24"
G	Filler-short	2	¾ × 1½ × 21"
H	Diamond	4	¾ × 1½ × 12"
I	Base	2	1½ × 3½ × 48"

(all parts cedar)

TOOLS & MATERIALS

- ☐ Drill
- ☐ Power miter saw
- ☐ Tape measure
- ☐ Framing square
- ☐ 1 × 2" × 8 ft. cedar (10)
- ☐ 2 × 4" × 8 ft. cedar (1)
- ☐ 1¼" deck screws (stainless steel)
- ☐ ½ × 4½" galvanized lag bolts w/nuts and washers (3)

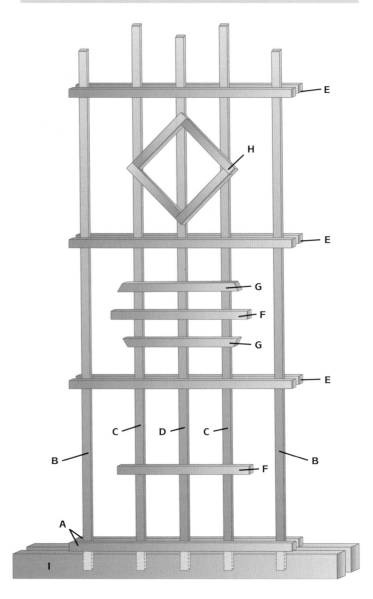

HOW TO BUILD A DIAMOND TRELLIS

Cut the uprights (also called stiles) and rails to length from 1 × 2 cedar furring strips. If your cedar stock has one rough face and one smooth, arrange the cut pieces so the faces all match.

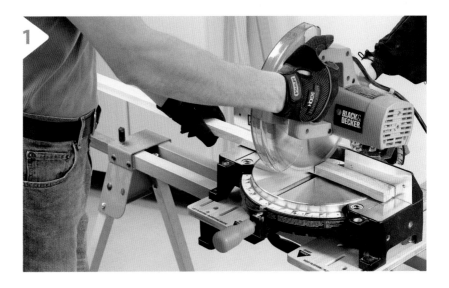

Lay the uprights on a flat surface with their bottom ends flush against a stop block and their edges touching. Draw reference lines across all five uprights to mark the bottom of each rail (the horizontal pieces). Measuring from the bottoms, rail marks should be at the following distances: 3", 33", 57", 82½"; unless, of course, you've redesigned the trellis for your needs.

Spread the uprights apart with the bottoms remaining flush against the stop block. The gaps between the outer rails and the inner rail should be 8"; the gaps between the inner rails and the center rail should be 6¼". Lay the rails across the uprights at the reference lines with equal overhangs at the ends. Drill a ³⁄₃₂" pilot hole through each rail where it crosses each upright.

4

Drive a 1¼" exterior screw at each pilot hole, taking care to keep the uprights and rails in alignment. Tip: Use stainless steel screws; they will not rust, corrode, or cause the wood to discolor. Overdrive the screw slightly so the screwhead is recessed.

Flip the assembly over once you have driven a screw at each joint on the front face. Position the second set of rails so their tops are flush with the first rails and their ends align. Drill pilot holes at each joint. Offset the pilot hole by ½" so the screws do not run into the screws driven from the other side. Drive screws to attach all four rails.

Attach the filler strips to the front side of the trellis according to the spacing on the diagram (page 46). Drill pilot holes so the filler strips don't split. The beveled ends of the short filler strips should be cut at around a 30° angle with a power miter saw or miter box.

5

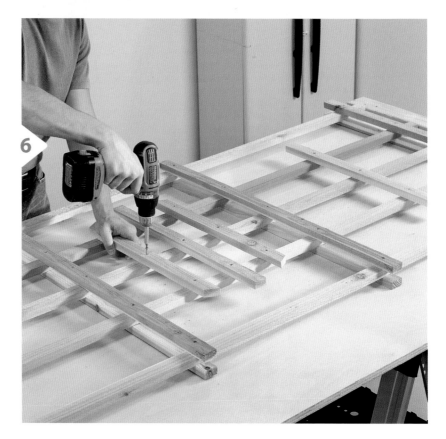

6

7. Make the decorative diamond appliqué. Cut four pieces of 1 × 2 to 12" long. Then, arrange the sticks into a diamond shape, with the end of each stick flush with the outer edge of the adjoining one. Drill a pilot hole and drive a screw at each joint. Attach the diamond shape to the top section of uprights, centered from side to side. Take care to avoid screw collisions in the diamond legs.

Install the base parts. The two-part 2 × 4 base seen here allows the trellis to be semi-freestanding. If it is located next to a structure you probably won't need to anchor the base to the ground, although you can use landscape spikes or pieces of rebar to anchor it if you wish. Cut the base parts to length and bolt them together, sandwiching the bottom 3" of the uprights. Move the trellis to your garden.

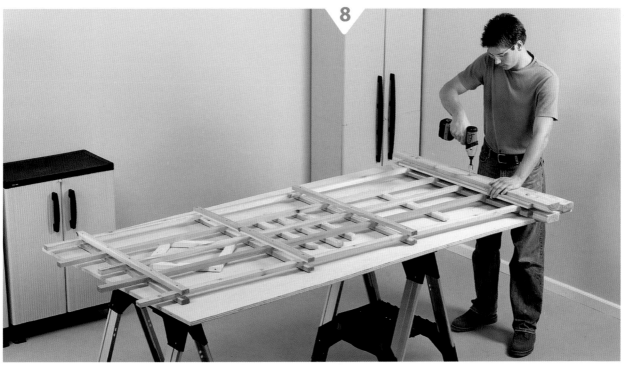

■ Finishing Your Trellis

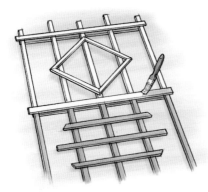

Trellises made from cedar can be left unfinished to weather naturally, coated with a UV-protecting exterior stain to enhance the wood tones, or painted. A bright coat of white paint will give your trellis visual lift; black paint works well too, giving the trellis an Asian design feel and also allowing it to recede so your plants are the star attraction.

IVY TOPIARY

A symmetrical, manicured topiary must be trimmed weekly to keep it from looking unkempt. When well maintained, though, it brings formality and visual appeal to your yard or garden.

If you prefer tidy over untamed, and manicured over messy, a topiary planting is a suitable selection for your space. In a way, topiary is the poodle haircut of shrubs. But the angular, clean appeal is artistic and lends itself to geometric garden designs.

You can achieve this look with a shortcut: create an ivy topiary from mature plants. The interesting container feature complements formal patio settings, or add a partner and flank your front door with two eye-catching topiaries.

Topiaries grow as fast as any plant, but you must be careful to trim them regularly so they don't lose their painstakingly neat shapes. The risk you take when trimming existing shrubs into unnatural forms is that excessive pruning, which is necessary for topiaries, can block light and oxygen from the center of the shrub. The result is an ornamental with lots of leaves on the surface, but nothing but naked branches in the guts of the shrub. In the long term, this is not especially beneficial for plants.

However, with proper plant nutrition—water, healthy soil, and fertilization—shrub topiaries will thrive in their sculpted forms. Topiaries that are pruned regularly, and this may mean weekly depending on the weather and type of plant, will look like living statues in a garden.

This particular project involves manipulating ivy into a three-tiered topiary. The structure is provided by round wire frames—you can buy these in craft stores or bend your own from flexible copper tubing. The trailing plant clings and grows to this form, thereby avoiding the pruning health problem discussed earlier. Pruning regularly, and never allowing ivy shoots to exceed 3 inches, encourages branching. This refers to offshoot growth that develops from pruned branch tips. The result: a rich, green topiary with interesting texture, thanks to ivy's distinct foliage.

You can find ivy in garden centers at almost any time of year. For instant gratification with this project, purchase mature hanging baskets of ivy that have about two dozen hanging stems. This plant will serve as the base inside the topiary frames.

TOOLS & MATERIALS

- **Large planting container**
- **Potting soil**
- **Gravel (for drainage)**
- **Wire topiary frames; two circles and a base**
- **One mature hanging basket of ivy**

A topiary is any leafy plant that is trained in a very neat manner around a trellis that functions as a skeleton. Two or three globe shapes mounted on a rod that's embedded in a container are really all you need to make a topiary like this.

HOW TO MAKE AN IVY TOPIARY

1 Prepare the planter or other container by spreading a layer of gravel for drainage and adding potting soil. Remove the ivy from the hanging basket and transfer to the container.

2 Assemble the wire frame according to the directions if it is a kit from the craft store; otherwise, bend ¼" flexible copper tubing. Embed the post (a piece of ¾" rigid copper tubing or piece of closet rod) into the planting container and attach one wire frame globe shape.

3 Wind the inner strands of the ivy around the wire frame. Allow the outer strands to drape over the side of the container.

4 After the ivy growth reaches the first globe frame, remove the leaves from the trunk area of the topiary.

5 Continue to train the ivy by trimming shoots that grow longer than 3". This will encourage branching and lush growth so the ivy will fill the topiary frame.

RAISED BED WITH REMOVABLE TRELLIS

A raised bed box made from 2 x 6 lumber is used as the base for a sturdy built-in trellis made of PVC tubing. It is perfect for climbing plants like beans or cucumbers.

For adding a trellis to a simple raised bed, it's hard to beat PVC plumbing pipe. It's inexpensive and rot-proof and goes together like pieces of a toy construction set. This all-purpose trellis is made almost entirely with PVC parts and is designed to be custom-fit to your raised bed. For a bed with 2x lumber sides, you can secure the trellis uprights to the outside of the bed with metal pipe straps. If the sides of the bed are built with timbers, the trellis simply drops into holes drilled into the tops of the timbers.

The trellis as shown is made with 1½" PVC pipe and fittings. The parts are friction fit only, so they are not glued together and can be disassembled easily for the off-season. PVC pipe and fittings are manufactured for a very tight fit; if you push the pipe all the way into the fittings, the joints won't come apart unless you want them to. Separate the joints by twisting the pipe or fitting while pulling straight out. Due to the tight fit, it doesn't help to try to wiggle it loose.

PVC pipe and fittings come in one color: stark white. You may want to paint your trellis to blend in with your garden setting, but this isn't required. Exposure to sunlight somewhat dulls PVC over time, but this doesn't significantly affect its strength.

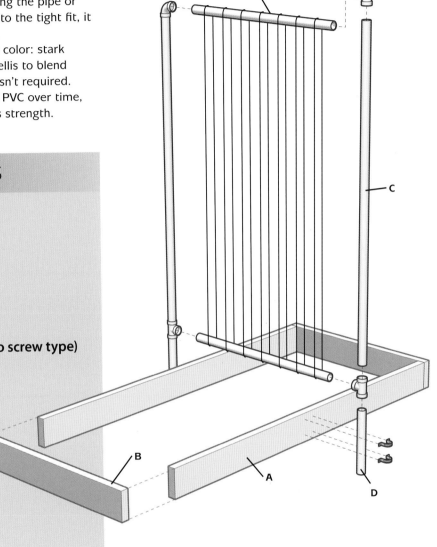

TOOLS & MATERIALS

- [ ] 1½" x 10 ft. PVC pipe (2)
- [ ] 1½" PVC 90° elbows (2)
- [ ] 1½" PVC T-fittings (2)
- [ ] Heavy jute or hemp twine
- [ ] 2 x 6" x 8 ft. cedar (1)
- [ ] 2 x 6" x 12 ft. cedar (1)
- [ ] Pipe straps for 1½" PVC (two screw type)
- [ ] Metal inside corners
- [ ] 1¼" deck screws (1 lb.)
- [ ] 2½" deck screws (1 lb.)
- [ ] Tape measure
- [ ] Drill
- [ ] Hacksaw or miter saw
- [ ] Sandpaper
- [ ] Scissors or utility knife

CUTTING LIST

KEY	PART	DIMENSION	PCS.	MATERIAL
A	Sides	2 x 6 x 72"	2	Cedar
B	Ends	2 x 6 x 36"	2	Cedar
C	Upper verticals	1½ x 60"	2	PVC
D	Lower verticals	1½ x 12"	2	PVC
E	Crosspieces	1½ x 34"	2	PVC

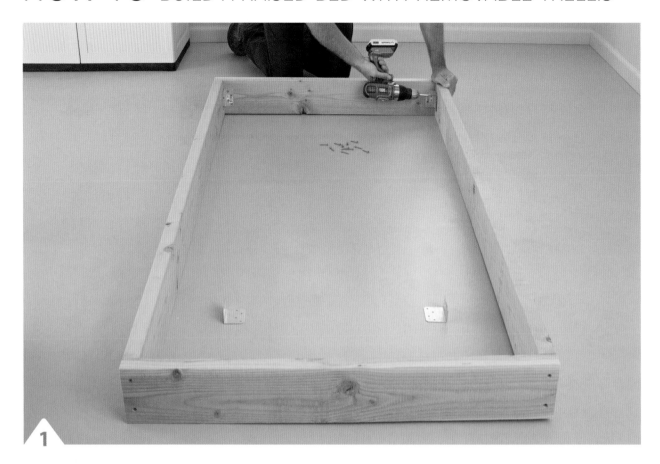

Start the project by assembling the 2 x 6 box (we used cedar), reinforcing the joints with metal inside corners. Add a center divider to keep the sides from spreading apart if you decide to make this project longer than 6 ft. Even if it is shorter, the divider is still a good precaution though.

Cut 12"-long pieces of 1½" PVC tubing. Attach them to the outsides of the planter box, near the middle. Use emery paper or sandpaper to remove the burrs and smooth the cut ends of pipe. Draw a perpendicular line where the pipe will go, using a square. Strap the pieces to the outsides with two pipe straps each. Fasten one strap with two screws, but leave the other strap loose until you put the upper vertical PVC on and can check it for plumb. Add a T-fitting to the top end of each pipe.

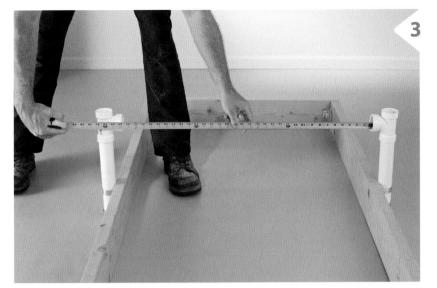

3 Measure between the hubs of the T-fittings, measuring to the insides of the sockets. Cut a piece of 1½" PVC pipe to this length and sand the cut edges smooth; this is the bottom cross piece. Remove both T's, fit the piece into the middle hubs of the T's so the ends of the pipe bottom out in the fittings, then put the T's back in place.

4 Add the uprights, then cut the top crosspiece and attach it with elbows. Make sure the pipes are plumb, then finish fully attaching the bottom straps to the planter box. Move the planter into your yard or garden and fill it with planting medium. Line the planter box with a thick layer of old newspaper or landscape fabric first. The last step is to tie jute or hemp twine to the crosspieces so that climbing plants have something to grab on to. When winter comes, you can disassemble the PVC and store it away until spring.

BENT BRANCH TRELLISES

Small branches, sticks and twigs normally end up in a drop off site for yard waste or perhaps a bonfire. The trellis projects on the following pages will show you how this "yard waste" can be converted to beautiful, useful garden furnishings. A few bent branch projects in the Planters chapter will give you even more options for this fun and creative way to build.

Designed and built by noted Canadian artist Dawn King, the stick projects seen here are surefire conversation starters and quite beautiful in their own right. Any versions you make will not look exactly alike, but that is one of the beauties of this method of furniture making. No two pieces are ever alike. As you gain experience you will start to see the potential in each stick or branch or twig you gather and you will find ways to create a design for it that plays to that potential. But for now, here are six wonderful garden trellis projects made with branches, sticks and twigs. Do your best to replicate one or more of them and you will be well on your way to becoming an experienced artist.

Bending twigs and branches into sturdy garden furnishings demands some creativity and patience, but the joinery methods are really quite simple and it won't take you long to get the hang of it. The results can be quite stunning and fit beautifully into just about any garden setting.

A CRASH COURSE
IN BUILDING WITH BRANCHES

By their nature, rustic projects will require rustic joinery techniques. Don't expect to get the kind of perfect, tight-fitting joints that are used in fine woodworking. There are three basic joining techniques. Most of the trellis and planter projects in this book can be made using just two of the techniques: face joints and sculpted face joints. The third type, mortise-and-tenon joints, are useful for tables and chairs and other highly-stressed furnishings, but you can get by without them when making trellises and planters.

FACE JOINTS are made by fastening one piece of wood directly on top of another. At the juncture of the two, you drill two pilot holes as far apart from each other as possible in the allotted space and then put a nail or screw into one hole to hold the two pieces together while other joints are made. When all joints have one screw in them, make sure the pieces are exactly where they should be, and everything is squared up. Then secure the shape by putting in, permanently, the second nail or screw.

SCULPTED FACE JOINTS give a tighter fit. They are created by grinding a hollow in the first piece of wood, so the second piece will fit snugly into it. An electric angle grinder can be used to sculpt a hollow very quickly and accurately. It is easiest to use this sculpting technique working from the front of a piece, but if you do, the nail or screw head will show. Sometimes this is fine, but for a fancier piece, try to work from the back or the inside of a piece, so the nails and screws do not show. It is fussier work, but gives a higher quality appearance.

Building rustic branch furnishings requires just a few basic tools, but a broad, flat work surface is a must.

■ Tools You'll Need

You can make just about every project in this section with this basic tool set, which includes (clockwise from top left) a power drill, a stapler, a cordless drill, a bypass pruning shears, a pruning saw, and a hammer. Once you get the fever, though, you may find additional tools helpful.

TIPS FOR BUILDING WITH BRANCHES

Use an electric angle grinder fitted with a bonded abrasive cutting wheel to "sculpt" a hollow in one of the mating branches. This is an aggressive power tool, so make sure your workpiece is secured well, especially if you are sculpting on the end of a branch as seen here. In some cases you'll sculpt a hollow in the side of a branch where another branch crosses it. Angle grinders (a 3.5" disc model is big enough for any of the jobs you see here) are not expensive, but you can rent a professional-grade one inexpensively if you don't want to take a chance on buying an entry level tool.

"Getting the spite out" is the traditional term for the technique of softening and flexing a thin, pliable branch so it is easier to bend and shape in projects that require branches that curve or bend in large sweeps. Flexing the branch back and forth helps soften and tenderize the wood fibers so they bend easily, and makes it less likely you'll break the branch when attaching it to your project.

A basic face joint is made by simply laying the mating branches across one another in the configuration you want and then securing the joint with a pair of screws. Always drill a pilot hole first to prevent the branches from splitting when you drive the screw (screws tend to have a much better holding power for these projects—deck screws are perfect with their coarse threads). When assembling a larger project, a good trick is to use just one screw per joint as you assemble, avoiding tightening it all the way. Then, once all of the joints are tacked together and everything looks great you can drive the screws all the way and then add a second screw to each joint.

Trimming the ends of branches, sticks, and twigs with a sharp knife keeps the bark from catching and peeling and makes for a neater finished appearance.

Gather together a supply of pieces before you start, and sort them by shape and size. This is much easier than trying to harvest individual pieces as you need them for a project. This is the corner outside Dawn's workshop where she stores straight pieces of varying sizes.

Be on the lookout for branches, sticks, and twigs with unique features and interesting figure.

GATHERING MATERIALS

The branches, vines, and small trees you'll need to build these projects are quite easy to come by and are usually free for the asking. If you live in a rural area, any woods or brush thicket where you have permission to cut green wood will provide all the materials you need. But even if you live in the city, suitable branches are easy to forage. Neighbors pruning trees or hedges likely will be happy to have you cart away materials they will have to dispose of anyway. Each thunderstorm may deliver a harvest of furniture building materials in the form of branches dropped by the wind.

Park maintenance people can be an especially good source of materials. They may even appreciate some help with their work. Many towns will have a yard waste depot at the municipal dump.

The rustic garden projects shown here are built from green wood— the branches must have been freshly cut from a living tree. Be sure to follow some basic rules when collecting materials. Ask for permission from property owners to harvest materials. Most people are quite fine about that; as long as you are taking only what they offer you are really doing them a favor. Often, your neighbors will be quite pleased that you're offering to clear away brush. But be sure to remember to give thanks for what you take.

POT TRELLIS

This basic bent branch trellis is designed to be used in conjunction with a planting container, but you can put it directly in the ground too.

Container gardens are so popular because they're easy to grow and maintain, but they can be a little boring if everything is the same height. When you add a trellis to a pot or other container, you add height to the display. It can also be planted in the ground as a garden accent among growing plants.

These rustic pot trellises are ideal for climbing vines of all sorts. A large trellis could support ivy, morning glories, or honeysuckle. A slightly smaller version would be an ideal companion for sweet peas.

One thought about shape and scale before we start: This trellis is designed to fan out to the sides. To create this shape, you need a range of curved sticks, some more curved than others. Try to arrange the sticks in a basic fan shape, but don't worry too much about making it perfect. The beauty of these projects lies in their unique character.

- Pruning saw or sharp pruning shears
- Sharp knife, such as a sturdy pocketknife
- Power drill
- Assorted screws
- Center post: straight branch ½" to ¾" in diameter, of chosen length (1) (ours is about 30")

- Inner slats: gently curved branches, 4" to 6" shorter than center post (2)
- Outer slats: severely curved branches, 4" to 6" shorter than center post (2)
- Bottom brace: straight branch, about 6" long (1)
- Arches: curved branches, (about 24" long) (2)

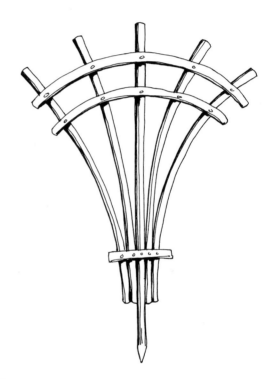

1 Select a straight stick as a center post, then whittle it to a point at one end. Lay one of the inner slats on each side of the center post, starting 6" to 8" above the pointed end. Put one of the outer slats on each side of the inner slats. (The curves of each stick should point away from the center stick.)

2 Cut a bottom brace and position it across the base of the trellis body, 4" to 5" above the ends of the slats. Drill pilot holes and screw the brace in place. Lay the arches across the fan of the trellis, a few inches down from the top. Drill pilot holes and screw these in place, too.

FRAME TRELLIS

This idea for a trellis is basically a nod to the art of gatebuilding. It is really just a sturdy frame with sticks for infill.

The base of this trellis needs to be straight; however, the top can be straight, arched, or any shape you find interesting. It can be any size you want too, so there are no specific measurements in the materials list. Unless it's going be fastened to a wall, the top doesn't need to lie flat, so this trellis may be an opportunity to use an unusual piece that isn't suitable for other projects.

Because of its size, this trellis needs quite a bit of support built into it. The frame can be decorated with branches and vines, but don't use small branches if you'll be removing dead vines in the fall. Include diagonals in your design to provide bracing and prevent "racking," or loss of shape. Secure the diagonals to the framework and to each other. The diagonal bracing can be provided by small angled branches that fork off from the vertical posts, as you see in this photo. In the project directions, though, you'll see how to add these supports after the vertical posts are installed.

If you use vines for decoration, or branches from a softwood tree, remember that they may need to be replaced after a few years. Cedar and hardwood branches tend to last longer than softer woods. Also, the thicker the branches are, the longer they will last.

TOOLS & MATERIALS

- Hammer, shears, and staple gun (optional)
- Poles: straight branches of chosen length (4 or 5)
- Bottom rail: straight branch of chosen length (1)
- Top rail: curved branch (1)
- Vines or branches (optional)
- Assorted screws, nails, and staples
- Power drill

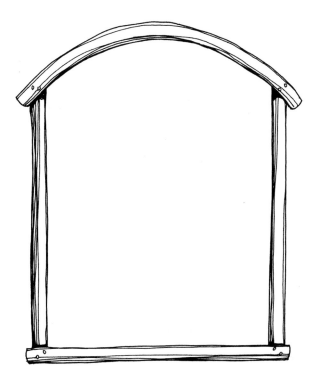

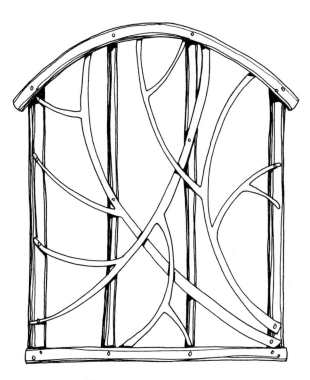

1 Lay the poles and the top and bottom rails on the ground or a large table, and drill two pilot holes as far apart as possible at each joint. Drive one screw into each joint. Make sure the sides are perpendicular to the base and put in the second screws. (If you're ready for more advanced designs, you may not want the sides to be perpendicular, but we're starting with a simple design here.)

2 If the trellis is a small- to medium-sized one, go ahead and decorate it now. If it's large, add two or three braces between the top and bottom rails. As you add decorations, arrange the branches to create diagonals and triangular bracing. Drive screws to attach the branches to one another as well as to the frame and braces.

FAN TRELLIS

The classic fan trellis form goes rustic when it is made with bent branches. The result is quite beautiful.

This trellis is not quite as easy to build as it looks. The biggest challenge is finding branches with just the right curves. While they can be bent a bit and held where you want with screws, it's important not to put too much stress on your trellis or it will twist and bend out of shape. Eastern white cedar is great wood for this because its branches grow in long, graceful curves, such as the ones you need for this project.

While this is a fairly classic design, it lends itself to many variations. You may want to play around with it and see what you can add to the basic design.

- Power drill
- Pruning saw
- Pruning shears
- Assorted screws
- Center post: straight branch of chosen length about 1" in diameter at base (1)
- Slats: curved posts, equal in size to center post (4)
- Arches: curved branches of chosen length (2)
- Bottom brace: straight stick, chosen to fit (1)

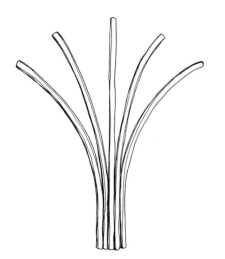
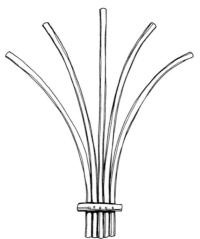
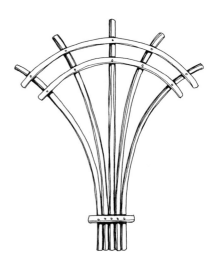
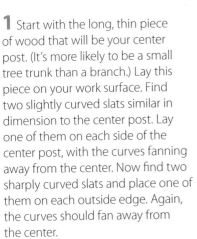

1 Start with the long, thin piece of wood that will be your center post. (It's more likely to be a small tree trunk than a branch.) Lay this piece on your work surface. Find two slightly curved slats similar in dimension to the center post. Lay one of them on each side of the center post, with the curves fanning away from the center. Now find two sharply curved slats and place one of them on each outside edge. Again, the curves should fan away from the center.

2 Now you need a short bottom brace similar in thickness to the base of the pieces already in place. It needs to be long enough to span the base of the trellis with a bit hanging over on each side. Put this brace across the base of the fan, a nice distance up from the bottom. Drill pilot holes and screw the brace into place. Make sure your screws are long enough to go deeply into the fan pieces, as this is a place where they tend to pull apart.

3 Find two matching arches that are similar in dimension to the other pieces of the trellis. Place them across the fan, near the ends. Drill pilot holes and drive screws into the joints to hold the braces in place.

LADDER TRELLIS

What better furnishing for your climbing plants than a ladder? This branch-built project definitely brings some whimsy into your garden.

This project is designed to lean against a wall or fence. Besides being a great support for plants, a ladder trellis can break up the monotony of a large, blank wall, or provide a decorative focus between a pair of windows.

A trellis can be attached directly to the wall or leaned up against it. If you attach it to a building, put spacers behind the branches so they don't sit directly on the siding. Make spacers by attaching small pieces of plastic or copper plumbing tubing to the trellis.

If you lean the trellis against a wall, anchor it well. You can drive wooden stakes, iron rebar, or steel T-bar (used as posts for wire fencing) into the ground beside the ladder poles and attach the poles to them. Secure wooden stakes to the trellis with long screws; wrap wire tightly around the poles and the rebar or T-bar. One good reason to secure the ladder trellis is that your kids will be less likely to haul it off and use it to get up on to the garage roof.

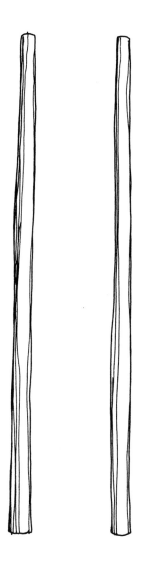

1 Lay the posts side by side with the bottoms even. Mark them at 1 ft. intervals, starting at the base. Cut six 14" rungs. (The rungs can be similar in size to your poles or slightly smaller.)

2 Place the rungs between the poles at the marks. Drill pilot holes through the sides of the poles and into the rungs. Attach the rungs with long, strong screws. If the ladder doesn't feel solid, add some bracing. Decorate the poles and rungs with twigs or vines.

VEGETABLE TRELLIS

Borrowing design principles from the lean-to, this basic plan is easy to re-size and modify.

The number of ways to use this vegetable trellis design are practically unlimited. On a tall version like this one you can grow heritage tomatoes, because they get to be 8 or 9 feet tall. You can build a shorter version to support pickling cucumbers. Build your trellises so that they can be easily moved whenever you rotate the use of your planting beds, as well as for storage over the winter.

When planning a trellis, match its size to its purpose and to the vegetables you'll be growing. Many trellises are built too small for their intended use. Perennial vines continue to grow almost indefinitely, and even annuals grow 10 to 20 feet in a summer.

This is a very simple plan: a tall tripod at each end of the trellis supports the horizontal rails that run from end to end.

1 Take two long legs and lay them on your work surface so that they make a V at the top. This V will be the support for one of your crosspieces. At the place where they cross, drill two pilot holes spaced as far apart as possible. Drive deck screws into the pilot holes to join the pieces.

2 Starting at the base, mark both poles at 1-ft. intervals. Then, cut the braces that will span the distance between the two poles, creating an A-frame ladder effect. Drill pilot holes and drive screws into the joints to hold the braces in place.

3 Stand the piece up and add a third leg to create a tripod. The top of this pole needs to sit to one side of the other two so it doesn't fill the space at the top. The top crosspiece will fit in that space. Repeat steps 1 through 3 to make a second tripod.

TOOLS & MATERIALS

- **Power drill**
- **Handsaw**
- **Legs: straight poles of desired height (we used 7-ft. legs) (6)**
- **Rails: straight poles of equal length (6)**
- **Braces: straight poles of various lengths (10)**
- **Assorted screws**

4 Place rails between the tripods. Attach each rail to the braces. The length of these poles will be determined by how you plan to use the trellis. Keep in mind that the poles will sag if they span too great a distance. Choose stout poles or add a brace in the middle of the span.

OBELISKS

The obelisk is undoubtedly the quintessential trellis shape. It is really just four legs meeting in a point at the top and supporting whichever crossmembers you wish.

Obelisks look glorious in a garden, rising grandly above other garden structures. You'll see them made from a whole host of building materials, including 2 x 2 lumber, copper tubing, even sections of drainpipe. They're very handy for supporting long vines and tall plants. If you live in an open area, be forewarned that obelisks can really catch the wind. To anchor an obelisk, pound a couple of long stakes into the ground and wire them to the centers of the crosspieces.

A fun tip: In the winter, decorate your obelisk with fresh greens and small lights for a festive touch in the garden.

TOOLS & MATERIALS

- ☐ **Power drill**
- ☐ **Hammer**
- ☐ **Saw**
- ☐ **Pruning shears**
- ☐ **Staple gun**
- ☐ **Legs: 7-ft. poles of similar thickness (4)**
- ☐ **Braces: 20" branches (2)**
- ☐ **Branches or vines**
- ☐ **Assorted nails, screws, and staples**

1 Lay two of the 7-ft. legs on the worktable with the bases aligned with the edge of the table and about 2 ft. apart. Cross the tops of the poles, creating a slight "X." At the juncture, drill two pilot holes as far apart as possible and drive screws into them. Place a 20" brace between the two poles, parallel to the edge of the table. Drill pilot holes in from the side, through the first leg and into the center of the 20" brace; drive a strong screw into the joint. Fasten the other end of the brace to the second leg.

2 Stand the frame upright. (You'll probably have to prop it against the worktable.) Place the base of the third leg about a foot away from the table edge, centered between the other two legs. Lay the top of the pole at the top of the frame. Drill pilot holes and fasten the third leg to the others.

3 Move the frame away from the table and add the fourth leg as described in Step 2. Put the other 20" brace (which may need to be cut a bit shorter), between the third and fourth poles, resting on top of the original brace. Drill pilot holes and drive screws through the third and fourth legs and into this brace. Where the two braces meet, drill two pilot holes as far apart as possible and drive screws into the joint.

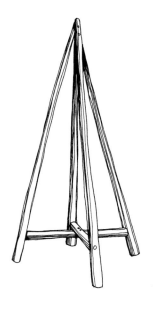

4 Decorate the obelisk with branches or vines. Cedar branches can be fastened at angles going up the obelisk. Or, mark the legs at one-foot intervals, wrap a thick grapevine in a spiral from the base to the top and then wrap another vine in a spiral from the other direction.

PLANTERS

Planters are used to grow and display plants anywhere around or inside your house, and they can be built almost any size, from small and portable to large and fixed in place. Planters allow you to transform otherwise barren areas like decks and porches and patios into lush gardens where you can grow most of the same flowers and veggies and ornamental plants that you can in a conventional garden or raised bed. Smaller planters or planters on wheels can also be moved to follow the sun, or be brought indoors during cold weather months—which gives northern gardeners the opportunity to enjoy plants from warmer climate zones that otherwise would not survive.

Most planters are made from wood, but other materials like metal or concrete or stone can also be used, either by themselves or with wood. For instance, the Garden Tower on page 84 combines a wooden base with metal buckets and threaded metal rod to create a distinctive planter that's still light enough to move around, while the Hypertufa Planter on page 110 is made from cement mixed with sphagnum moss and other additives.

There are two basic types of planters, though some can be used either way. Designs like the Twisted Planter (page 78) and the Stick Tripod Planter (page 126) are built as containers for potted plants; the wooden frame doesn't come in contact with soil and water just drips through the bottom. The other type of planter is built to be filled with soil and planted—much like a miniature garden. These can be quite large, like the Pallet Planter on page 102, or small and easy to move like the Mini Planter (page 81). You can compromise, to some extent, between the two types with a design like the Coffee Table Planter (page 122), which is built to fit a certain size pot or container, but the size of these is limited to containers that can be lifted in and out easily.

Both types have their advantages. The type used for potted plants will last much longer, since there's no soil contact, and it's simple to switch plants for a different, fresher look. However, plastic or clay pots sitting inside a wood enclosure don't look quite as good when viewed from close up. The type filled with soil looks nicer up close, and can be built as large or as small as you'd like, and in any shape that you can figure out how to build. However, unless it's made from a rot-proof material like hypertufa or lined with metal or rubber liner, it will eventually rot, though pressure-treated wood will last longer than cedar or redwood.

Whatever type you choose, planters are a great way to enjoy your flowers and plants. Most are simple and fun to build, and in just a few hours you can enjoy your favorite flowers, herbs, or veggies anywhere in the house.

TILED PLANTER BOX

A few nonwood items will add some variety to your yard or garden furnishing. Here, ordinary floor tile is used to clad a wooden planter box.

This planter box is decorated with 12 x 12" floor tiles that are bonded to the box sides as cladding. Because tile comes in so many colors and textures, your decorative options when using it are virtually unlimited. You can select ceramic, porcelain, or natural stone tiles. The dimensions provided work with 11⅞" square slate tiles with tight joints and no grout. You can use other size tiles, but you'll need to modify the dimensions of the parts. If you plan on leaving the planter outdoors and exposed to the elements, use epoxy mortar to affix the tile and epoxy grout, to fill the gaps between tiles. All of the tile products needed are available at any tile store and at most home centers.

TOOLS & MATERIALS

- 2 x 4" x 8-ft. exterior wood (1)
- 1 x 4" x 8-ft. exterior wood (3)
- 2" deck screws (1 lb.)
- 2" galvanized finish nails (1 lb.)
- 12 x 12" tiles (6)
- Drill
- Saw

- Margin trowel
- ½"-thick x 3- x 5-ft. cement backer board (1)
- Thinset mortar for 6 square feet (Use epoxy mortar if planter will be outside in freezing temperatures.)
- Exterior grade epoxy grout (optional, depending on tile)
- Notched trowel (buy ¼ x ⅜" or size recommended for your tile on mortar bag)

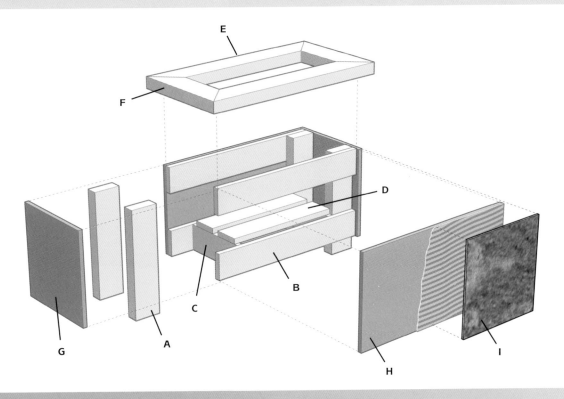

CUTTING LIST

KEY	PART	DIMENSION	PCS.	MATERIAL
A	Legs	1½ x 3½ x 14"	4	Rot-resistant wood
B	Rails	¾ x 3½ x 22"	4	
C	Inside supports	¾ x 3½ x 11"	2	
D	Bottom boards	¾ x 3½ x 16"	2	
E	Long cap boards	1½ x 3½ x 25"	2	
F	Short cap boards	1½ x 3½ x 14"	2	
G	Tile backer board	½ x 11¾ x 11¾"	2	Tile backer
H	Tile backer board	½ x 11¾ x 21¾"	2	
I	Tiles	11⅞ x 11⅞"	6	Tile

HOW TO MAKE A TILED PLANTER BOX

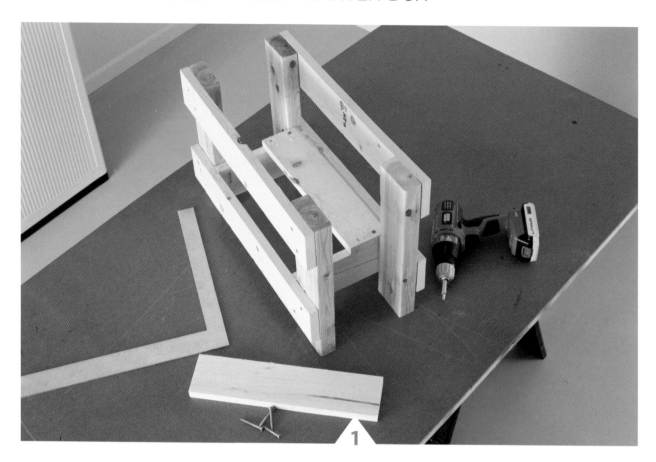

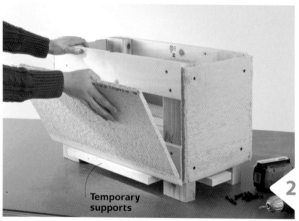

Temporary supports

Cut the legs and rails to length. Attach the bottom rails to the legs with 2" exterior-rated screws. Next, attach the side rails to the legs with 2" screws. Drive the screws so that the heads are flush or slightly below the surface of the wood. Connect the sides with the inside supports, then add the bottom boards. Align the inside supports with the rails, then set the bottom boards in and fasten them. Tip: It's a good idea to check the size of the tile you've selected to make sure the rails are not set too low or high.

Attach the backer boards and tile. The tiles will be attached to cement tile backer board. Measure the size for the backer, but then deduct ¼" to allow for rough edges. For example, if the measurement is 12 x 12", cut the backer 11¾" square. Use a utility knife to score along each line. Then snap the backer board and use the utility knife to score through the backside of the board. Before attaching the backer board, screw temporary supports to the bottom of the rails, extending them at least an inch beyond the frame so the tile will be even around the bottom edge and well-supported while the mortar sets up. Attach the backer board to the legs and side rails with 1¼" screws. Keep the smooth factory edge of the backer board down, so that the bottom edge of the planter will be smooth.

3 Attach the tile to the backer board. Use the recommended trowel size for the tile you buy (it will be listed on the bag of mortar) to apply the thinset or epoxy mortar to the backer boards. Set the tiles on the temporary supports and press them into place, tapping them lightly with a rubber mallet or your fist so they fully adhere. If you're making the corners tight, without grout, you may need to adjust one of the sides by adding more mortar to the back of the tile. Use epoxy mortar if the planter will be outdoors through the winter.

4 After the mortar has set up for several hours, attach the cap boards to the frame with 8d x 2½" galvanized finish nails. Cut the cap boards with a power miter saw or handsaw and miter box. The cap boards should overhang the outside of the side rails and legs by 1½", which creates a ½" ledge overhanging the tile. To measure the cap boards, find the distance from the outside of the wood frame to the outside of the wood frame and add 3". This distance will be the long edge of the miter cut. Apply exterior stain or sealer to the frame and cap boards. Select a stain color that complements the tiles. Remove the temporary supports and set the finished planter in place.

■ A note about tile

Measure the tile you select before building the frame, so you don't end up with big gaps at the corners, especially if you're using 12" square tiles without grout. The actual size of a 12" tile may only be 11⅞", which means the total finished size would only be 23¾ x 11⅞" plus the thickness of the tile and mortar. The Cutting List on page 75 is for tile that's 11⅞" square x ⅜" thick, and assumes that the mortar will add about ⅛". If you use a smaller tile with grout, figuring out the dimensions will be a little easier because you can adjust the grout lines to make up small differences. Buy a tile with nice-looking outside edges, since the edges will be exposed, or use bullnose tiles, which have a finished edge. Natural stone tile is usually a good choice.

TWISTED PLANTER

Made from square wood frames that are stacked in a uniformly offset pattern this planter will add a little motion and drama to your garden.

Although the Twisted Planter has a unique appearance that makes it seem complicated to build, the construction is based on a simple trick—just offset each layer. Inspired by the elegant twisted chimneys sometime seen on old houses, this planter will take a little longer to build than a conventional wood box (figure about half a day with screws, or less with a finish nail gun), but the extra effort produces a piece that will have people asking "How did you do that?"

The entire planter is made from 18" square cedar frames stacked on top of each other. We used 15" and 18" lengths to build frames with some exposed end grain, but if you prefer not to see end grain you can miter the corners, in which case all the lengths would be 18". The plant supports at the bottom of the planter are also made from 2 x 2 cedar, although you could substitute 1 x 2 cedar or pressure-treated wood.

Before you start cutting, measure the exact width of the 2 x 2s. They're called 2 x 2s, but they're actually 1½ x 1½"—except sometimes they're really 1⁷⁄₁₆" square, and occasionally even smaller. Who knows why. But, unless you're mitering the corners, it matters, because if you don't add that extra ⅛" to the 15" pieces so that the boxes are exactly square, the twisting edges won't line up quite as well.

■ **Tip**

For the best results, clamp a stop block to your miter saw table (or set up a jig if you're using a circular saw) so that all the pieces come out the same size. Cut all the long pieces, then move the stop block and cut the short pieces.

CUTTING LIST

DIMENSION	PCS.	MATERIAL
2 x 2 x 18"	20	Cedar
2 x 2 x 15"	22	
2 x 2 x 14¼"	5	

TOOLS & MATERIALS

- [ ] 2¼" exterior-grade, self-drilling trimhead screws (2 lb.)
- [ ] 2 x 2" x 8-ft. cedar (9)
- [ ] Square bit for screws
- [ ] Clamps
- [ ] Saw
- [ ] Drill

HOW TO MAKE A TWISTED PLANTER

Assemble all the 2 x 2 frames first, joining the pieces with a single trimhead screw at each corner. For quick, accurate assembly, clamp or screw two straight boards to the edge of your work table. Use a framing square to make sure the boards are perpendicular to each other. Then, assemble the 2 x 2s against the boards and screw them together with self-drilling trim head screws, which look attractive, go in easily, and almost never split the wood. Regular deck screws can also be used, but you'll need to drill pilot holes first. To make very fast work of it, use a pneumatic finish nailer with 2½" galvanized or stainless steel nails. Assemble all the frames. Sand any dirt or roughness off the boxes before you begin stacking them.

To support the plant container that will go inside the planter, build a base support from 2 x 2s. Double the 15" pieces on the first level box, then add crosspieces to the inside of the second level. Cut the crosspieces 14¼" long to avoid the twisting second level.

Now the fun part. The twisting effect is created very simply, by offsetting each level ½". Start at any corner and make a mark ½" towards the next corner. Repeat for each corner, using light pencil marks that won't be visible after the next layer is on. Place a new 2 x 2 frame on the previous one and line up the corners with the marks. Line up the sides from layer to layer so that all the 18" pieces are on the same side; the corners won't look right if the 2 x 2 ends appear and disappear from layer to layer. Continue until you run out of frames. With a little fine-tuning, all the corners will line up with the marks. Drive two screws into each side about 4" from each edge. The screws won't be visible after the next layer is on, so you can use less-expensive deck screws, though you should predrill if the cedar shows signs of cracking.

Add small, nail-on feet (nylon furniture glides are shown here) to keep the base off the ground so water can drain through. If you keep the planter indoors, put a shallow pan under the center to catch drips. Finish the planter with an exterior stain or clear finish.

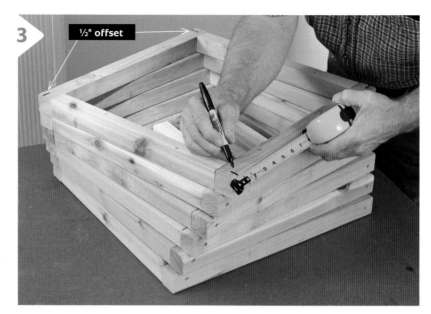

½" offset

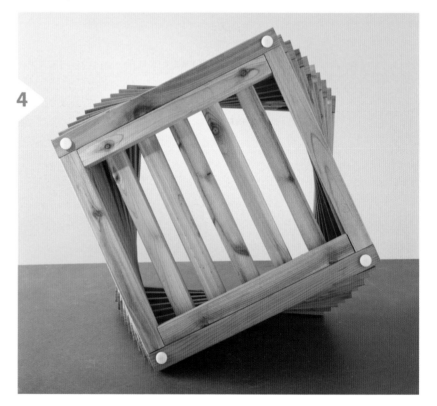

MINI PLANTER

Need some small planters to fill in spaces around a deck or patio? The mini planter is a simple design that's perfect for flowers and small herb gardens, and easy enough to build that beginners can tackle it. It's compact and light enough that you can easily move it around for better sunshine or a different look, or bring it indoors when the temperature drops. Still, it holds enough soil to support several healthy plants. Made from a single 12-ft. long 2 x 4 and a small piece of metal flashing, the mini planters go together so quickly that you can build half a dozen in the morning, paint or finish them in the afternoon (if you want to), and fill them with plants the next day.

Planters can be set out by themselves, placed on outdoor shelves or walls, or stacked in pyramids or other stepped designs—the thick sides and 2 x 4 legs offer plenty of support. However, if you stack them more than three high, fasten them together with small metal straps or mending plates just to be on the safe side.

The construction is very simple, but for the best results it's important to square all the pieces, align the screws with each other and predrill all the screws. On small pieces of wood like this, screws can easily start splits when they're driven straight in, although they might not show up for a year or two. *(continued next page)*

Built from small pieces of 2 x 4, these little planters can be mixed and matched and combined to meet just about any garden, porch or patio needs you may have. And they are very easy to make.

TOOLS & MATERIALS (per box)

- [ ] 2 x 4" x 12-ft. cedar or other rot-resistant wood
- [ ] 15 x 9" aluminum or galvanized flashing
- [ ] 2½" deck screws (1 lb.)
- [ ] 1" stainless steel pan head screws (10)
- [ ] Landscape fabric
- [ ] Drill
- [ ] Countersink bit
- [ ] ¼" metal drill bit
- [ ] Saw
- [ ] Leather gloves

CUTTING LIST

PART	DIMENSION	PCS.	MATERIAL
Front	2 x 4 x 13"	4	Cedar
Legs	2 x 4 x 9"	4	Cedar
Sides	2 x 4 x 8"	4	Cedar

HOW TO MAKE MINI PLANTERS

To start, cut all the pieces using a stop block or cut multiple pieces together so that all the legs and sides are the exact same size. Select the best sides of the legs and front pieces, then lay the legs out, good side down, and draw lines 1" from the inside edge of each leg. Place the front pieces on the line so they overlap 1" onto the back of the legs and flush with the top. Predrill the screws at a slight angle toward the center of the leg for more strength. Use two screws per board. Assemble both the front and the back of the planter.

Attach the side pieces to the legs and the front by driving one screw through each side piece into the matching front board, then one screw per board through the front into the sides. Predrill all the screws. Space the screws in the front symmetrically for a neater appearance. Make sure to offset the screws by ½" so that they don't all go into the same spot in the leg.

The last step is to cut the metal bottom to size and attach it. Galvanized metal has to be cut with tin snips, but aluminum flashing can be cut with several passes of a razor knife. Wear leather gloves to protect against sharp edges and metal splinters. Place the metal on a piece of scrap wood and drill six ¼" dia. holes for drainage. Screw the metal to all sides of the bottom of the planter with 1" screws. Sand the outside and either leave the wood natural or finish it with a penetrating oil or paint. The inside should be left unfinished. Then cut a piece of landscape fabric or screen mesh the size of the inside of the box and set it in the bottom to cover the holes so that dirt won't fall out. Make a few more of the planters if you like, then fill them with dirt, add plants, and set them outside in the sun.

GARDEN TOWER

Three galvanized metal buckets and a piece of threaded rod are the primary components of this simple planter that is a terrific conversation starter.

Ever thought about vertical container gardening? This creative project speaks for itself in terms of look and function, but what might need some explanation is how the tower is put together. It's surprisingly simple: The main structure is a long piece of threaded rod, or "all-thread," that's secured to a plywood base with washers and nuts. The bottom (largest) bucket gets a large hole that fits over a nut on top of the base.

The remaining buckets each get a smaller hole sized for the all-thread, and the bucket is secured to the rod with washers and nuts below and above the bucket's bottom. You tighten the nuts toward each other so they clamp together, sandwiching the bucket. An added benefit of this system is that it's adjustable; you simply thread the nuts up or down as desired to change the spacing of each bucket.

Drainage holes drilled into the bottoms of the buckets allow each container to drain into the one below it, while the lowest bucket has holes on its outside wall. Aluminum screening inside the buckets keeps soil from escaping through the drainage holes.

The project as shown uses three buckets—a large (20 quart), medium (12 quart), and small (5 quart). You can use the same number and size of buckets as shown or go with a slightly smaller or larger size range, or even add another small bucket at the top. Buckets are sold at most hardware stores and home centers, although stores with an agricultural focus tend to have the best selection.

TOOLS & MATERIALS

- Galvanized buckets (3), large, medium, and small
- ¾" plywood, 16 x 16" minimum
- 1 x 2" x 8-ft. pressure-treated wood
- Exterior paint or polyurethane and finishing supplies
- ⅝"-dia. x 48"-long zinc or galvanized threaded rod
- (8) ⅝" x 2"-O.D. zinc or galvanized flat washers
- (8) ⅝" zinc or galvanized nuts
- Drill and metal cutting bits up to ⅝"
- Finish nail and string or wood strip
- (2) Adjustable wrenches

- Exterior wood glue
- 1¼" deck screws
- Landscape fabric
- Sandpaper
- Jigsaw
- Clamps
- Hacksaw
- Utility knife
- Aviation snips
- Permanent marker

HOW TO MAKE A GARDEN TOWER

1 To start, mark a 16"-dia. circle onto the less appealing side of a piece of ¾" plywood (power jigsaws cut on the upstroke, so the nicer surface will have less tear-out). This will be the planter base. Use a home-made string compass to lay out the circle; just drive a nail in the center of the square piece of plywood and then tie an 8+"-long piece of string to the nail. Tie a pencil to the other string end so it is 8" from the nail. Rotate the pencil around the nail to draw the 16"-dia. circle.

2 Drill a ⅝" hole (the guide hole for the threaded rod) at the center of the plywood. Cut out the circular base with a jigsaw and a smooth-cutting wood blade, then sand the edges smooth. Cut six 8" lengths of 1 x 2; these will be the feet for the base. Lay the 1 x 2 feet out symmetrically on the underside of the plywood, leaving them ¼" back from the edges. Outline the feet on the plywood, then remove them, predrill two screw holes in each, and squirt a bead of wood glue on the back edges. Fasten the feet with 1¼" deck screws. At this point, finish the entire base with stain, spar varnish, or paint. Let the finish dry completely.

Determine the length of the threaded rod you need by adding up the heights of the buckets, plus 20 to 24" for the two spaces between buckets, plus 2½". Cut the ⅝" threaded rod to length at this dimension, using a hacksaw. For the design and buckets shown here, use a 42" rod and space the buckets 11" apart. Tip: Thread a ⅝" nut onto the threaded rod, going well past the cutting line so it won't interfere with your saw. Once the rod is cut, unthread the nut all the way from the rod; this helps straighten any threads damaged by the cutting. Add a nut and 2" washer to one end of the rod, then fit the rod end through the hole in the plywood base. Add a washer and nut on the underside of the base and tighten the nuts toward each other. Stand the base and rod upright. Drill a ⅝" hole down through the center of the largest bucket. Enlarge the hole just enough to fit over the upper nut on the planter base.

Drill four or more ¼" drainage holes along the perimeter of the bucket through the outside wall just above the bucket's bottom (not the bottom edge). Fit the bucket down onto the rod so it rests on the plywood base; this bucket doesn't need to be secured to the rod.

Add a nut followed by a washer to the rod, and thread the nut down to 10 to 12" above the first bucket.

Drill ⅝" holes in the center of both smaller buckets, along with four ¼". drainage holes in the bottoms of the smaller buckets. Slide the second bucket down, thread a washer and nut on, and tighten the nuts against each other. Add landscape fabric to cover the holes. Repeat for the third bucket, leaving an inch or so of threaded rod projecting through the bottom of the top bucket. Finally, move the tower into position and fill the buckets with potting and plants. Add the two smaller buckets to the rod. Lock the buckets in place with a washer and nut below and above the bottom of the bucket.

STEPPING STONE
PLANTER/TABLE

Have some leftover tiles, flagstone (even the plastic kind!) and wood lying around your garage that you don't know what to do with? Try building a small planter table with your excess materials. This attractive table can be built in just a few hours. The main requirement is that the top is more or less flat and that you have the tools to cut a hole in it. If you are an ambitious type or have access to large stone-cutting saws and tools, just pick a nice piece of flagstone and cut your own hole wherever you want it. Or, buy a stone at your landscape supplier and see if you can get them to cut the hole for you. However you proceed, please be advised that cutting a large hole in a piece of dense natural stone is a big project in and of itself. In the project seen here, we cheated. We bought an artificial plastic

These little garden accent tables feature large flat stones (or artificial stepping stones as shown here) with a circular cutout that works like a giant cupholder for a 6″ pot.

(continued next page)

stepping stone from a local garden center. Unlike a real stone, an artificial stone can be cut and shaped quite easily using normal woodworking tools.

To cut this imitation flagstone we used a smooth-cutting jigsaw blade (a plastic-cutting blade also works), but you can cut a similar hole in tile, marble, or flagstone with masonry drill bits and a diamond-grit jigsaw blade (available at most home centers and hardware stores). For rectangular cuts, you can also use an angle grinder or even a circular saw; diamond blades are available for either, and are relatively inexpensive. But, as stated earlier, this can be more work.

TOOLS & MATERIALS

- **Plastic or natural flagstone, tile, or wood (any size above 16")**
- **Plant container with taper or lip**
- **4 x 4 x 12" rot resistant wood (4)**
- **Caulk**
- **2½" deck screws (1 lb.)**
- **1 x 3" x 8-ft. rot-resistant wood**
- **2 x 6" x 2-ft. rot-resistant wood**
- **Mosaic stone tile (Optional: 4 or more)**

■ Shopping Tip

Shop around for just the right round container. The container you choose must have a substantial loadbearing lip (preferably with a horizontal ledge that can rest on the tabletop) along its top edge so the container can be suspended from the tabletop surface. A substantial lip also helps hide any chips or other imperfections along the hole's edges. The material of the pot does not really matter—lightweight plastic works just as well (or even better) than fired clay or ceramic pots.

HOW TO MAKE A STEPPING STONE PLANTER/TABLE

Cut the parts for the wood table base. After the top is cut, build a base from four 12"-long 4 x 4s and a 1 x 3 rail with (optional) mitered corners. Measure the stone top, then cut the rails the same size. Set the 4 x 4s upside down on the worktable and attach them with screws or nails. You can use the base as it is, or as an option add 1½ x 4 x 4" feet. Attach the feet with two predrilled screws—be sure to drill a generous hole for the screws so they don't split the feet when you set them. The feet limit the amount of moisture that is drawn up into the end grain of the legs.

2

Prepare the underside of the top, if it is artificial stone, before it is attached to the table. Trim off any plastic knobs or teeth that are meant to grab the ground. A sharp utility knife is the best tool for trimming these parts.

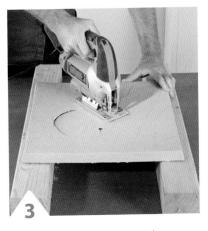

3

Turn the pot or planter upside down on the top, or on a cardboard template if you're working with rough stone, and trace the rim. Draw another line inside that one representing the width of the pot's lip. Using a jigsaw and fine-tooth blade, cut out the circular hole for the planter into the top piece. The cut should stop just short of the cutting line (⅛" or so), leaving enough lip that the pot will hang securely from the top but can still be easily removed.

4

Flip the base over and set the top onto it. For a plastic top, just drill a hole at each corner and fasten the top to each leg with a single screw. For stone or tile, you can either drill a hole or glue the stone to the wood base with polyurethane construction adhesive. As an optional final touch, cover each screwhead with small stone mosaic tiles, attaching the tiles with clear or matching color acrylic caulk. Otherwise, just dab a little caulk over each screwhead.

A well-designed planter table or plant display table can look great even when they're constructed from ordinary, construction-grade materials. This table gets its charm from the way the pressure-treated 1 x 2s—usually not a very attractive material—are turned on edge.

BAMBOO BUNDLE PLANTER

A piece of 3 to 4"-dia. bamboo cane cut into random lengths and bundled together is really all there is to making this Tiki-style planter.

Real bamboo pole makes a great planting vessel, for several reasons. It's a plant itself (a grass, technically) and can be used in its natural form with no sealants or protectants required. It's relatively decay-resistant and holds up well to moisture and outdoor exposure. And it's easy to work with using standard workshop tools.

This simple planter can be made from an 8-ft. length of 3", 4", or 5" diameter bamboo. As shown here, the pieces are held together with twine and a few dabs of clear caulk, but you can bundle your poles with the twine alone if the pieces fit together well, allowing you to separate the sections for easier planting or to bring some plants inside or give them a little more or less sun than the others.

Large bamboo poles are cut from the "trunk," properly called the culm, of the bamboo plant. The culm is made up of segments, each separated by a joint, or node, which includes a solid disc of material inside the culm that gives the plant structural stability. When making a planter, the bottom of each planter vessel must include an intact node to contain the soil, while the top segment must be open at the top and include a sufficiently long hollow area for planting. Holes are drilled through the bottom and any intermediate nodes to provide drainage.

Since all of the planter sections are the same diameter, a bundle requires seven pieces total: one center piece surrounded by six additional pieces. You can use any lengths you like: the design shown here has pieces that range from 4" to 22" long. It is okay to have more than one piece the same length, just try not to put them next to one another. You can arrange the pieces in any order. Once you have a basic design nailed down, roughly lay out the necessary cuts on your bamboo to make sure you'll have enough to complete your design.

TOOLS & MATERIALS

- **3"- or 4"-dia. x 8-ft. bamboo pole (or equivalent in shorter pieces)**
- **Clear silicon caulk/adhesive (optional)**
- **Waxed lashing twine (or hemp or jute twine)**
- **Hacksaw, handsaw, or miter saw**
- **Drill and ½" bit**
- **Sandpaper**
- **Band clamp or tie-down strap**

■ Buying Bamboo

You can purchase bamboo pole in a variety of sizes and finishes through some import/export retail shops, larger garden centers, as well as from online retailers. If you need to have the material shipped to your home, ask about having it cut down to smaller sizes for shipping. Online retailers often cut long poles for a small fee, but the money saved on shipping makes this a good option.

■ Cutting Bamboo

Bamboo is a surprisingly hard material, largely because of the fibers that help to make it strong. But these fibers also make bamboo tricky to cut smoothly. To prevent the outer skin of the bamboo from splintering when you cut it, wrap the bamboo pole with masking tape in the rough area where you will cut it. Mark your cutting line onto the masking tape and then make the cut. After you remove the tape, resist the urge to sand the cut edges—in most cases this will only disturb the fibers more and make the cut rougher. If you are not happy with the smoothness of your cut, use a sharp utility knife to gently whittle the cut ends smooth. Cleanly cutting the fiber ends works much better than trying to grind them smooth with sandpaper. You can also use a miter saw, but clamp the pieces firmly to the fence before cutting.

Cut the bamboo pieces to length according to your design, using a hacksaw, handsaw, or miter saw. Draw a continuous cutting line by wrapping the bamboo with a straight piece of paper; align the side edges of the paper on your mark, then trace along the paper to make the line. Remember that each planter section must have a node to hold the soil. Tip: To prevent tear-out and splintering, wrap masking tape around the circumference of the pole before making the cut. Drill holes with a ½" spade bit through the nodes for drainage. For this plan, we cut the bamboo into 4-, 6-, 10-, 13-, 15-, 18-, and 22-inch pieces, but you can use any sizes that look good.

Tip: As a decorative alternative to a straight cut, you can bevel the top ends of the poles, cutting them at any angle you like. You can use a jigsaw or coping saw to cut waves or other shapes into the top edges, if desired.

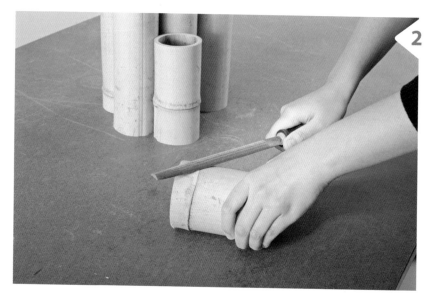

2 Dry-assemble the bamboo pieces until you find an arrangement that pleases you. File down any very pronounced nodes in the area where they will butt against another piece of bamboo—this improves the fit by making the parts flush. Also try spinning the bamboo pieces to find the spot where the profiles match best—the poles are usually a little wider in one direction.

Bottom node

3 If a piece has two nodes, you may have to break one out. Drill one or more holes with a large drill bit or hole saw to make room for the soil and plant roots. Drill a ½" hole in each node for drainage, then drop in a circle of aluminum screen or landscape fabric to hold the soil in.

4 Tie a decorative band of jute or hemp twine around the planter assembly. To prevent soil from falling through the drainage holes, cover each bottom node with a disc of landscape fabric or insect screening before adding soil. Finally, wrap the bamboo tightly with hemp or jute twine, winding the twine around so that each wrap sits neatly on top of the one before it. Black waxed lashing twine is a traditional material used to bind bamboo joints, while hemp or jute has a coloring that's more similar to natural bamboo— either choice will look good. Tip: When you add soil to each pole, only add it to within 1" of the top. If you overfill it, mud will run out when the planter is watered and the planter will look very dirty.

PLANTER BOXES

Decorating a garden is much like decorating a room in your home—it's nice to have pieces that are adaptable enough that you can move them around occasionally and create a completely new look. After all, most of us can't buy new furniture every time we get tired of the way our living rooms look. And we can't build or buy new garden furnishings every time we want to rearrange the garden.

That's one of the reasons this trio of planter boxes works so well. In addition to being handsome—especially when flowers are bursting out of them—they're incredibly adaptable. You can follow these plans to build a terrific trio of planter boxes that will go well with each other and will complement most gardens, patios, and decks. Or you can tailor the plans to suit your needs.

Whatever the dimensions of the boxes, the basic construction steps are the same. If you decide to alter the designs, take a little time to figure out the new dimensions and sketch plans. Then devise a new cutting list and do some planning so you can make efficient use of materials. To save cutting time, clamp together parts that are the same size and shape and cut them as a group (called gang cutting).

When your planter boxes have worn out their welcome in one spot, you can easily move them to another, perhaps with a fresh coat of stain, and add new plantings. You can even use the taller boxes to showcase outdoor relief sculptures—a kind of alfresco sculpture gallery.

(continued next page)

Whether you build only one, two, three or twenty, these handy cedar planters are small enough to move around your gardens and inside your greenhouse or garden shed. The basic construction is the same for all three models shown here—just the size and shape change.

TOOLS & MATERIALS

- Tape measure
- 8-ft. cedar 1 × 2s (3)
- 6d galvanized finish nails
- 8-ft. cedar 1 × 4s (6)
- 4 × 8-ft. sheet of ⅝"
  T1-11 siding
- 2 × 4-ft. piece ¾"
  CDX plywood
- Deck screws (1¼", 1½")
- Circular saw
- Exterior wood stain
- Straightedge
- Paintbrush
- Eye and ear protection
- Finishing sander
- Work gloves
- Miter box and backsaw
- Drill

CUTTING LIST

KEY	NO.	PART	BOX A	BOX B	BOX C	MATERIAL
A	2	End panel	⅝ × 15 × 11⅛"	⅝ × 15 × 17⅛"	⅝ × 15 × 23⅛"	Siding
B	2	Side panel	⅝ × 22¼ × 11⅛"	⅝ × 10¼ × 17⅛"	⅝ × 10¼ × 23⅛"	Siding
C	8	Corner trim	⅞ × 3½ × 11⅛"	⅞ × 3½ × 17⅛""	⅞ × 3½ × 23⅛"	Cedar
D	2	Bottom trim	⅞ × 3½ × 9¼"	⅞ × 3½ × 9¼"	⅞ × 3½ × 9¼"	Cedar
E	2	Bottom trim	⅞ × 3½ × 17"	⅞ × 3½ × 5"	⅞ × 3½ × 5"	Cedar
F	2	Top cap	⅞ × 1½ × 18"	⅞ × 1½ × 18"	⅞ × 1½ × 18"	Cedar
G	2	Top cap	⅞ × 1½ × 24"	⅞ × 1½ × 12"	⅞ × 1½ × 12"	Cedar
H	1	Bottom panel	¾ × 14½ × 19½"	¾ × 14½ × 8½"	¾ × 14½ × 8½"	Plywood
I	2	Cleat	⅞ × 1½ × 12"	⅞ × 1½ × 12"	⅞ × 1½ × 12"	Cedar

Note: Measurements reflect the actual size of dimension lumber.

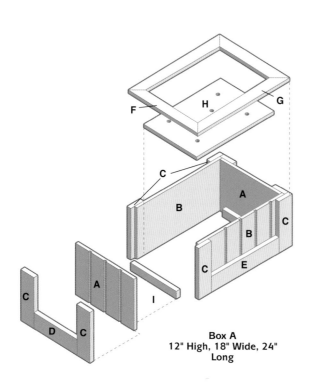

Box A
12" High, 18" Wide, 24" Long

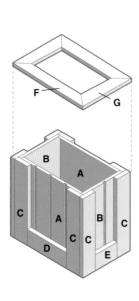

Box B
18" High, 18" Wide, 12" Long

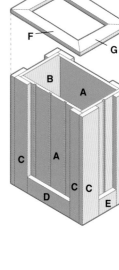

Box C
24" High, 18" Wide, 12" Long

HOW TO BUILD PLANTER BOXES

1 Cut all the wood parts to size for the first box you're making, according to the dimensions in the Cutting List on page 94. Use a circular saw and a straightedge cutting guide to cut the T1-11 siding panels (if you have access to a tablesaw or a panel cutter you can use that instead).

2 Assemble the box frame. Place the end panel face down and butt it against a side panel. Mark the locations of several fasteners on the side panel. Drill 3⁄32"-dia. pilot holes in the side panel at the marked locations and fasten the side panel to the end panel with 1½" deck screws. Fasten the opposite side panel the same way. Attach the other end panel with deck screws.

3 Attach the corner trim. Position one piece of corner trim flush to the corner edge and fasten to the panels with 1½" galvanized deck screws driven into the trim from the inside of the box. Place the second piece of trim flush to the edge of the first piece, creating a square butt joint. Attach to the panel with 1½" galvanized deck screws. For extra support, endnail the two trim pieces together at the corner with galvanized finish nails.

Attach the bottom trim. Fasten the bottom trim to the end and side panels, between the corner trim pieces and flush with the bottom of the box. Drive 1½" deck screws through the panels from the inside to fasten the trim pieces to the box.

Attach the cap pieces. Make 45° miter cuts at both ends of one cap piece, using a miter box and backsaw or a power miter saw. Tack this piece to the top end of the box, with the outside edges flush with the outer edges of the corner trim. Miter both ends of each piece and tack to the box to make a square corner with the previously installed piece. Once all caps are tacked in position and the miters are closed cleanly, attach the cap pieces using 6d galvanized finish nails.

Install the cleats to hold the box bottom in place. Screw to the inside of the end panels with 1½" deck screws. If your planter is extremely tall, fasten the cleats higher on the panels so you won't need as much soil to fill the box. If doing so, add cleats on the side panels as well for extra support.

7 Finish and install the bottom. Cut the bottom panel to size from ¾"-thick exterior-rated plywood. Drill several 1"-dia. drainage holes in the panel and set it onto the cleats. The bottom panel does not need to be fastened in place, but for extra strength, nail it to the cleats and box sides with galvanized finish nails.

8 Finish the box or boxes with wood sealer-preservative. When the finish has dried, line the planter box with landscape fabric, stapling it at the top of the box. Trim off the fabric at least a couple of inches below the top of the box. Add a 2" layer of gravel or stones, then fill with a 50/50 mix of potting soil and compost. Tip: Add wheels or casters to your planter boxes before filling them with soil. Be sure to use locking wheels or casters with brass or plastic housings.

▪ Tip

Play with the arrangement of your planter boxes. If you build one of each of the different sized boxes you can put them together soldier-style, stepping up by height. This will give a fairly formal look to the boxes. Or, you can get a little more freestyle with them, as in the photo on page 93. Because they share enough design elements, you can also put them far part and they will still coordinate nicely.

DRIP-DRY WASHTUB PLANTER

An original, customized planter should not be this easy to make, but it is. A 1-bushel galvanized tub set onto a pan of rocks makes an interesting and practical design statement. And it is on wheels!

If you've done any container planting you know that the vessels always need drainage. When the planters are indoors or on a patio or balcony where you don't want water running all over the place, you solve this problem with a little tray that fits neatly under your pot. But what if you want to do some serious container gardening, and pots just won't cut it? This easy-to-build tub planter employs the same convenient drip-tray system with a supersized container.

You can make your planter with any suitable rust-proof tub of any shape or size, as long as you can find a tray or pan that's a bit larger than the tub's bottom diameter. Washtubs and other vessels are available in a wide range of sizes, styles, and materials. You can shop online or browse local garden centers, hardware stores, and even farm suppliers for just the right combination of containers. The project shown here uses a 1-bushel galvanized steel washtub and a shallow, galvanized pan that has something to do with the keeping of hogs.

TOOLS & MATERIALS

- Large galvanized washtub (shape and size as desired)
- Galvanized or heavy-duty plastic wash pan or deep tray (sized to accommodate tub bottom)
- Finish nail and string or wood strip (for round planter pans)
- Aluminum window screen
- (4) swiveling casters with screws
- ½", ⅛", and ¹⁄₁₆" drill bits
- 80- or 100-grit sandpaper
- Small river rock
- ¾" plywood
- Permanent marker
- Drill
- Hammer
- Tape measure
- Aviation snips
- Jigsaw

Drawing circular cutting lines

To start, mark a circle on a piece of ¾" plywood the diameter of the bottom pan. This will be the planter base. Use a home-made string compass to lay out the circle; just drive a nail in the center of the square piece of plywood and then tie a piece of string to the nail. Tie a pencil to the other string end so it marks half the diameter of your base. Rotate the pencil around the nail to draw the circle.

Keep It Mobile

A large washtub full of soil, plants, and water can get very heavy, so this planter includes a sturdy plywood base that rolls around on swiveling casters. The base cart makes it easy to wheel the planter around on your patio or deck to catch the best sun; or you can give it a quick spin for a daily or weekly rotation. It also keeps the bottom of the planter off the floor, eliminating the potential for condensation or trapped rain water below the drip tub that could damage decking or patio surfaces or indoor flooring.

HOW TO MAKE A DRIP-DRY WASHTUB PLANTER

Drill ⅜" drainage holes about 4" apart in the bottom of the galvanized tub. Place scrap wood under the tub so the drill bit cuts through cleanly. Hold the tub tightly—it will spin around as the bit goes through the metal. To start, mark drainage holes in the bottom of the planter tub. Set the tub on top of a scrap of plywood or lumber. Working from inside the tub, punch a dimple or small hole at each mark with a punch or large nail and hammer. Drill a hole down through the bottom of the tub at each mark with a drill and ⅜" twist bit.

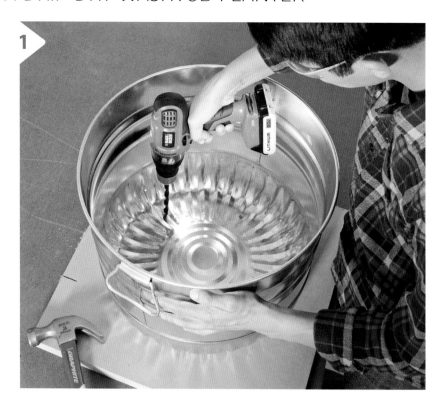

On a piece of ¾" plywood, lay out a circle the same diameter as your planned rolling base, (see Drawing Circles, page 99). Cut out the circle with a smooth-cutting jigsaw blade. The plywood should be cut so the pan fits over it, with no wood beyond the edge. Sand the edges and apply an exterior finish.

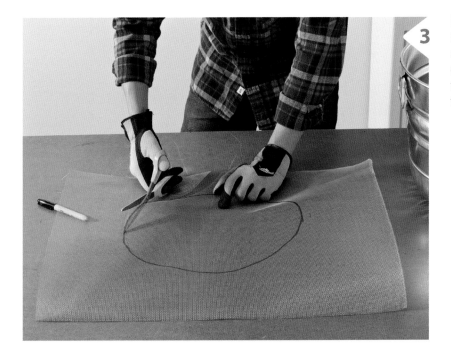

3 Insert a a piece of aluminum screen into the bottom of the tub. Cut the screen with aviation snips or heavy-duty scissors. Use the screen inside the tub to prevent soil from falling through the drain holes.

4 Space four swiveling casters evenly on the plywood 1" from the outside edge. Predrill and install the casters. Cover the bottom of the pan (not the washtub) with an even layer of small river rock or decorative gravel. Smooth out the rock to create a flat surface for the tub to rest on. Place the pan on top of the caster cart so it's centered over the plywood base, then set the tub onto the rock layer in the pan and add soil and plants.

■ **Tip**

To prevent overflowing the drain pan, add water to the tub's soil in small increments, giving the water a few minutes to filter through the soil before adding more.

UPRIGHT PALLET PLANTER

Pallets have come to be viewed as a legitimate resource for making items for the home and yard in recent years. In many cases, the pallet is broken up into individual boards and then reassembled. For this vertical planter project, the pallet is left intact and converted for use on a patio, deck, or balcony.

Pallets are so abundant in this country that they're often just left by the curb for people to take as firewood. Despite this lack of value, they can actually be quite useful—perfect for a wide variety of recycled wood projects like furniture, tables, wall coverings, flooring, chairs, artwork, and, yes, planters, and raised beds.

Since pallets have to carry thousands of pounds, they're generally made from tough hardwoods without big knots, and when the wood is cleaned up and sanded it can look surprisingly attractive. Pallet wood may not last as long outdoors as cedar or treated wood (unless you find a pallet made from white oak), but since it's free you can just replace it when it rots. In the meantime, it looks great.

There are many different ways to turn a pallet into a planter, but don't count on just pulling out all the nails and reusing all the pieces. It can be done, but hardwood grips nails a lot tighter than the softwoods used for construction lumber, and the wood slats often crack before the nail pulls out. Always grab a few extra pallets. If you have to remove a few pieces, lever carefully under the wood slats, and use a reciprocating saw outfitted with a metal-cutting blade to cut nails that are hard to pull. However, the easiest way to utilize pallets is to use them as is—which is what we're doing with our project. We designed this one to be vertical, but you can also lay it flat and stack a few underneath so that the plants are at a comfortable height, or combine several in a stairstep design.

Look for pallets in industrial and commercial areas. If you're lucky, you'll see a big pile with a "Free" sign on them, but you can also find them poking out of dumpsters or just piled up in a parking lot. If in doubt, just ask if you can take a few. Most will be dirty and have a cracked or missing slat, but if you grab an extra you can use it for parts. Avoid ones that look heavily oil-stained.

After brushing off the dirt and renailing any loose boards, put some 80-grit sandpaper on your sander and clean up the areas that will be visible. Also round over rough, splintery edges. Paint or finish the outside of the pallet, if desired, but don't do the inside if you're planting edibles.

Decide which end of the pallet will be up, then cut some cedar 2 x 2s and screw or nail one to the back edge each slat, except the bottom one (Photo 1). This will help keep dirt from falling out through the openings.

Fill the gaps on the sides with a strip of metal flashing, an extra slat or a piece of wood cut to size. Cover the back with rubber pond liner, aluminum coil

TOOLS & MATERIALS

- **Wood pallet**
- **2 x 2 x 8 ft. cedar (3)**
- **Scrap lumber (or [2] 1 x 4 x 8 #2 pine)**
- **Rubber pond liner or 6-mil black poly**
- **⅜" stainless steel staples**
- **80-grit sandpaper**
- **1⅝" deck screws (1 lb.)**
- **Drill and bits**
- **Power sander**
- **Saw**
- **Staple gun**
- **Potting soil**

stock or even a double layer of black 6-mil poly (but make sure none of it is exposed to the sun, or it will decay). Slide it in on the inside and nail or staple it to the edges with stainless steel staples so it stays in place (Photo 2). Add additional slats on the back to keep the soil from bulging out—inexpensive 1 x 4s or exterior plywood will work.

Finally, nail a doubled over strip of aluminum screen mesh across the bottom of the pallet to keep the dirt in, and then fill with top soil. Tamp it down with a long stick to make sure the pallet fills up. Dirt will fall out the front at first, but will settle in at an angle behind each opening.

Used wooden pallets destined for the dump can be found near factories and large retail stores, and are usually free for the taking (although you should always ask permission first, of course). Along with pallets that are in good general condition, look for ones made from hardwood—white oak is sometimes used for pallets because of its strength and durability. Most are lower grade woods, however.

HOW TO BUILD AN UPRIGHT PALLET PLANTER

Cut the 2 x 2 shelves to length and fit them in on the lower edge of each slat. Predrill and toenail at each end to hold them in place, then drive an additional screw into the cedar from the front. Pallet wood is hard, so predrill all screw holes. NOTE: Most pallets have a good face and a bad face. Be sure that you are creating your planter so the face with the nicer decking will point away from the wall you are installing it against. The pallet in Photo 1 has the less desirable side facing up.

You can use heavy black poly sheeting to make the liner, but for a more durable material use roll rubber. This thick rubber sheeting is sold as a roof covering or pond liner at most larger building centers or garden centers. But if you check with a local roofing company that installs rubber roofs you can probably pick up some scrap strips of rubber for free—that fits well with the pallet theme, anyway. Measure and cut the pond liner or poly for the back. Fold the liner onto the sides and staple it in place on the sides and back.

To stiffen the pallet and provide a surface for attaching the liner, fill the gaps on the back side with wood scraps of roughly the same thickness as the back boards.

■ Planting Your Pallet Planter

As you examine your completed pallet planter, one question immediately comes to mind: Won't all the dirt fall out the front? Well, if you did not plant any plants in it the answer is yes, it will. However, you are relying on the plant roots and the 2 x 2 shelves you installed to hold things together. To add plants, lay the planter flat on its back and plan to keep it that way for a couple of weeks. Pack the gaps full of potting soil (potting soil is pre-fertilized, unlike topsoil) and then pack in as many seedlings as you can fit. Water the plants for a couple of weeks so the roots can establish. Then, tip the planter up against the wall in position. A little soil may trickle out initially, but you should find that everything holds together nicely.

FREESTANDING WINDOW BOX

Adding a window box to your house adds charm and character and a splash of bright color, and it's also a great way to improve your house's curb appeal. In addition, it's an easy way to improve the view from the inside. But many people dismiss this project as impractical because they don't want to or can't attach the box to their house—a valid concern since any screws or nails that go into the window sill and siding have the potential to create problems with rot in the future. It's also a bad idea in general to make holes in aluminum or vinyl siding. The easiest solution to this dilemma is to simply mount the window box on posts that are set in the ground next to your house, but are not connected to the house at all. And by using unobtrusive 2 x 4s for the posts and planting climbing plants or bushes around the posts, you can easily make the posts disappear. Naturally, this planter is only appropriate for ground level windows.

This attractive project has all the features of a traditional window box, but without the biggest drawback: you don't have to puncture the outside walls of your house to hang it. It is designed to be supported solely from below.

(continued next page)

■ Tips for Making the Freestanding Window Box

Making these window boxes is an easy project. The only tools you need are a saw, a hammer or nail gun, and a drill driver. All of the parts for the planter box are cut from 1 x 8 boards of cedar, redwood, pressure-treated wood or other rot-resistant material, and making all of the parts is as simple as crosscutting these boards. A miter saw is the easiest type of saw to use for cutting the parts to size, but you can also use a portable power saw, such as a circular saw or jigsaw, and a straightedge to help guide the saw. Most lumberyards and home centers will also cut wood you purchase there for free or for a small fee.

HOW TO BUILD A FREESTANDING WINDOW BOX

Cut the five planter box parts to length. The box parts are all cut from cedar 1 x 8. As seen, the front board is a 37½" long, the back board is 36" long and the sides are 12½" long. The bottom panel is a 36"-long 1 x 8. The posts are 5-ft. long pieces of 2 x 4; they are sized for a 3-ft.-high window box, with two feet buried in the ground. No matter what height you need, always set the posts at least 2 ft. in the ground. You'll likely need to alter the lengths according to the height of your windowsills. You should also alter the front, back, and bottom board lengths to match your window width—the back and bottom boards should always be 1½" shorter than the front board. To assemble the box, start by attaching the back to the legs with construction glue and 2" deck screws. Next, attach the sides to the legs and the back. Use plenty of glue and several screws—the sides will be carrying all the weight.

2

Now attach the front and bottom pieces to the sides. Use construction glue and either predrilled 2" screws or galvanized finished nails. If you've enlarged the dimensions of the box to fit a larger window, add galvanized corner braces on the inside at the sides and center to reinforce the bottom. This design is sized to create a ¾" gap between the back and the bottom to allow excess water to drain out of the box. For a box that's longer than 3 ft., also add a corner brace in the center between the posts to keep the bottom from sagging over time.

¾" gap

3

After the box is constructed, cut a 4" strip of aluminum screen mesh or heavy-duty landscape fabric and staple it with stainless steel staples to the bottom and back. This will keep the dirt from falling out. Apply your finish of choice to the window box. If you used cedar as we did, you can leave the box unfinished to weather.

■ Install the window box

Mark the post positions on the ground in front of the window where the planter will be installed. Dig a 6"-dia. x 24"-deep hole for each post with a posthole digger. (Caution: Always be sure to call 811 to have the area checked for buried utilities and power lines before you dig deep holes in your yard. This is a free service.) Pour 2 or 3" of non-compactable gravel in the bottom of the holes to allow water to drain away from the post. Place the posts in the holes and have a helper hold them plumb and level as you fill around the posts with more gravel. Tamp the gravel firmly in place to keep the window box from sagging forward.

VARIATION: TRADITIONAL WALL-HUNG WINDOW BOX

Most window boxes are not freestanding like the one you've just seen built. For a more typical treatment, you can simply create a wood box and hang it from eyehooks beneath the windowsill.

Building a traditional wall-hung window box is very easy. The hard part is hanging it from the wall. This is especially true if your exterior walls are made of stucco or masonry. But even vinyl or steel siding can be a problem as most homeowners are reluctant to pierce the siding material. Luckily, the window box hanging strategy shown here lets you mount the box without penetrating the wall skin.

Build the Box

The size of your window box should be based on the size of the window it will grace. Because creating a window box involves converting wood pieces into a weather-ready outdoor home for plants, opt for rot-resistant wood, such as cedar or redwood. And take care to complete the finishing touches of this project, as they are critical to plant health. Your window box needs

TOOLS & MATERIALS

- Supplies
- 4-ft. 1 x 6 (1)
- 8-ft. 1 x 8 (1)
- Saw
- Drill
- ¾" drill bit
- Wood glue
- Sandpaper
- Landscape fabric
- Nonstaining (coated or stainless steel) deck screws
- Screwdriver
- Hooks and eye screws (at least 1½")
- Natural sealant, such as linseed oil or beeswax
- Exterior paint or finish

drainage holes and landscape fabric to prevent soil loss. Add to your window box's life expectancy by buying metal or plastic liners. Finally, play with the decorative possibilities by painting the window box to coordinate with your home.

The window box seen here is constructed from five boards with measurements based on a standard, single window. The box length should be ¾" wider than the window opening. This one is made using 1 x 8 boards for the front and back and 1 x 6 boards for the bottom and ends. You just cut the front, back, and bottom all to the same length and cut the end pieces to 1 x 8 width (7¼") minus ¾", for a cutting height of 6½". Drill pilot holes and screw the parts together. You can use exterior-rated wood glue to strengthen the joints but it is not necessary. Drill ¾"-dia. drainage holes in the bottom panel, spaced every 6".

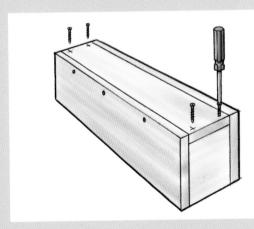

Hang the Box

Attach the box to the wood trim board beneath the window wherever possible. Attach a pair of exterior-rated screw eyes to this board, preferably at a wall-stud location. Attach screw hooks to the window box, aligned with the screw eye locations. Hang the hooks from the eyes and cut a pair of wood spacers to fit between the bottom edge of the box and the house siding. Glue the spacers to the back of the window box.

Tip: To keep the weight down, fill the box with a mixture that is equal parts potting soil and vermiculite.

HYPERTUFA PLANTER

A lightweight version of concrete, hypertufa is an easy material to work with and makes beautiful garden accessories.

Gardening magazines and catalogs often feature what appear to be stone or concrete troughs brimming with flowers or planted as alpine gardens. Often, these are made not with concrete but with a material called hypertufa. With hypertufa, you can create inexpensive, long-lasting planters that resemble aged stone sinks or troughs. Because the hypertufa mix uses lightweight soil amendment like perlite or vermiculite instead of heavy stone aggregate, hypertufa is light and manageable. You simply blend up the mix and pour it into a form where it sets up and cures. Hypertufa dries to the color of concrete. If you prefer another color, simply add concrete dye during the mixing process. Tinting products are very concentrated, so start with a small amount and add more if necessary.

Stocking the trellis planter is a matter of personal taste and growing conditions. In most areas, ivy, clematis and grapevines are good examples of climbing plants that can be trained up the trellis. Ask at your local gardening center for advice on plantings. You can set containers of plants in the bin or fill the bin with potting soil and then add plants.

TOOLS & MATERIALS

- [ ] (1) 2 × 6" × 8-ft, cedar
- [ ] (1) 2 × 4" × 6-ft. cedar
- [ ] (4) 2 × 2" × 8-ft. cedar
- [ ] (3) 1 × 6" × 8-ft. cedar
- [ ] (1) 1 × 2" × 6-ft. cedar
- [ ] Tape measure
- [ ] Drill
- [ ] Counterbore bit
- [ ] Jigsaw
- [ ] Compass
- [ ] Square
- [ ] Moisture-resistant glue
- [ ] 2" deck screws
- [ ] 1⅝" and 2½" deck screws
- [ ] Finishing materials

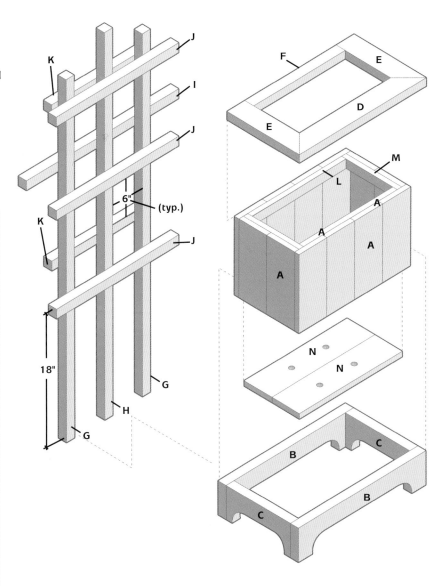

NOTES: Overall size: 69" high, 17¼" deep, 30" long • Measurements reflect the actual size of dimension lumber • Use cedar for all lumber

CUTTING LIST

KEY	NO.	PART	DIMENSION	KEY	NO.	PART	DIMENSION
A	12	Box slats	⅞ × 5½ × 13"	H	1	Center post	1½ × 1½ × 63½"
B	2	Base front, back	1½ × 5½ × 25"	I	1	Long rail	1½ × 1½ × 30"
C	2	Base ends	1½ × 5½ × 12¾"	J	3	Medium rails	1½ × 1½ × 24"
D	1	Cap front	1½ × 3½ × 25"	K	2	Short rails	1½ × 1½ × 18"
E	2	Cap ends	1½ × 3½ × 14¼"	L	2	Long cleats	⅞ × 1½ × 18½"
F	1	Cap back	1½ × 1½ × 18"	M	2	Short cleats	⅞ × 1½ × 11"
G	2	End posts	1½ × 1½ × 59½"	N	2	Bottom boards	⅞ × 5½ × 20¼"

HOW TO BUILD A TRELLIS PLANTER

Build the planter box. Cut the box slats and cleats to length. Arrange the slats edge-to-edge in two groups of four and two groups of two, with tops and bottoms flush. Center a long cleat at the top of each set of four slats, so the distance from each end of the cleat to the end of the panel is the same. Attach the cleats to the four-slat panels by driving 1⅝" deck screws through the cleats and into the slats. Lay the short cleats at the tops of the two-slat panels. Attach them to the slats the same way. Then, arrange all four panels into a box shape and apply moisture-resistant wood glue to the joints. Attach the panels by driving 1⅝" deck screws through the four-slat panels and into the ends of the two-slat panels.

Install the box bottom and base. Cut the bottom boards to length. Set the bin upside down on your work surface, and mark reference lines on the inside faces of the panels, ⅞" in from the bottom of the bin. Insert the bottom boards into the bin, aligned with the reference lines to create a ⅞" recess. Scraps of 1× cedar can be put beneath the bottom boards as spacers. Drill ⅛" pilot holes through the panels. Fasten the bottom boards by driving 1⅝" deck screws through the panels and into the edges and ends of the bottom boards. Make the base (optional) and attach it to the box bottom with 1⅝" deck screws driven through the planter box and into the base.

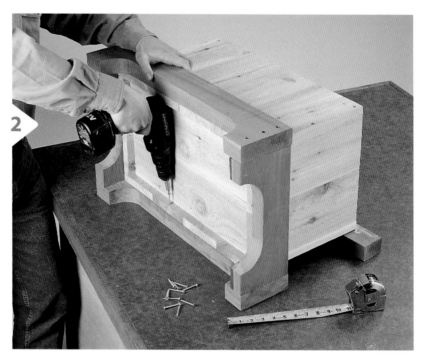

Making the Base

The planter base is scalloped to create feet at the corners. Cut the base front and back and the base ends to length. To draw the contours for the scallops on the front and back boards, set the point of a compass at the bottom edge of the base front, 5" in from one end. Set the compass to a 2½" radius and draw a curve to mark the curved end of the cutout. Draw a straight line to connect the tops of the curves, 2½" up from the bottom of the board, to complete the scalloped cutout. Make the cutout with a jigsaw, then sand any rough spots. Use the board as a template for marking a matching cutout on the base back. Draw a similar cutout on one base end, except with the point of the compass 3½" in from the ends. Cut out both end pieces with a jigsaw. Fasten the base ends between the base front and back by driving three evenly spaced deck screws at each joint.

3 Make the cap frame. Cut the cap front, cap ends, and cap back to length. Carefully cut 45° miters at one end of each cap end and at both ends of the cap front. Join the mitered corners by drilling pilot holes through the joints. Fasten the pieces with glue and 2½" deck screws. Clamp the cap front and cap ends to the front of your worktable to hold them while you drive the screws. Fasten the cap back between the cap ends with deck screws, making sure the back edges are flush. Set the cap frame on the planter box so the back edges are flush. Drive 2½" deck screws through the cap frame and into the side and end cleats.

4 Make the trellis from pieces of cedar 2 x 2 assembled in a crosshatch pattern. The exact number and placement of the pieces is up to you—you can use the same spacing shown here and on page 115, or create your own. Cut the end posts, center post, and rails to length. Lay the end posts and center post together side by side with their bottom edges flush so you can gang-mark the rail positions. Draw lines across all three posts, 18" up from the bottom; then 7½" up from the first. Draw additional lines across the posts, spaced 7½" apart. Cut two 7"-wide scrap blocks and use them as spacers to separate the posts as you assemble the trellis. Attach the rails to the posts with 2½" deck screws driven into pilot holes. Alternate from the fronts to the backs of the posts when installing the rails. Fasten the trellis to the back of the planter box. Finish as desired.

CEDAR PLATE
PLANTERS

These cedar planters are simple projects that can transform a plain plant container into an attractive outdoor accessory.

Add a decorative touch to your garden, deck, porch or patio with these stylish cedar planters. Created using square pieces of cedar fashioned together in different design patterns, the styles shown above feature circular cutouts that are sized to hold common sized pots and containers. If you have particular containers you would like to use with the planters you can adjust the hole size to match.

To build them, simply cut 1 x 10 cedar to 9¼" lengths, then make 7¼"-dia. (or another dimension if you choose) cutouts in the components as necessary. If you are making just a few planters, you can use a jigsaw to cut out the circles in each board. For a faster, production approach use a router and a template. Routers are not easy tools for beginners to use, though, so proceed with caution and practice on some scrap before you start cutting into your work pieces.

- 1 x 10" x 6-ft. cedar board
- ¼ x 20 x 20" hardboard or plywood
- Moisture-resistant glue
- 2" deck screws
- Pot, can, or other planting container
- Finishing materials

CUTTING LIST

KEY	PART	DIMENSION	MATERIAL
A	Component	¾ x 9¼ x 9¼"	Cedar

Number of pieces varies according to planter style.

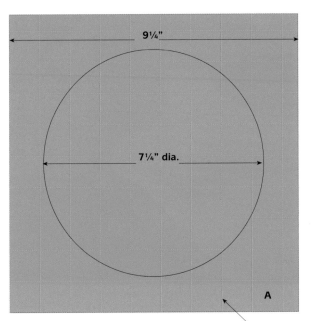

9¼"

7¼" dia.

A

Cutout Diagram   1" squares

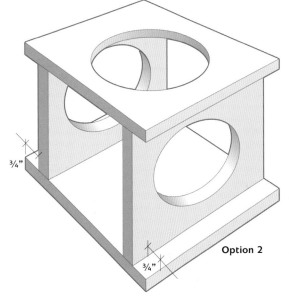

¾"

¾"

Option 2

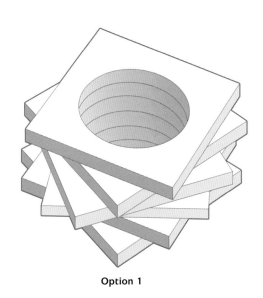

Option 1

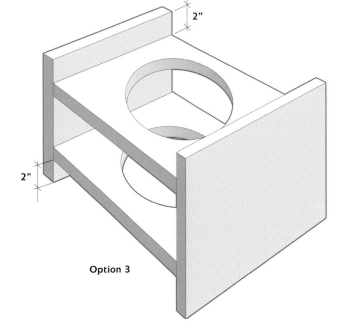

2"

2"

Option 3

HOW TO MAKE CEDAR PLATE PLANTERS

Spiral Stack Plates

Cut the number of cedar plates required for your design. Because 1 x 10 cedar is actually 9¼" wide, cut each piece to 9¼" long so the plates are exactly square. Make circular cutouts on those plates that require them. To do that, draw diagonal lines connecting the corners of the plates. The point of intersection is the center of the square board. Center a template, pot, can, container . . . whatever will fit into the planter, onto the component and trace it.

Use a drill to bore a ½"-dia. starter hole inside the circle you've drawn. Cut out the round waste piece with a jigsaw—use a blade with fairly big teeth. Cut just up to the line and then smooth your cut with sandpaper or a wood rasp. Then, use the first completed plate as a template for laying out the other round cutouts. Make

sure the edges of the piece you are marking are aligned with the edges of the finished piece and trace the cutout. Cut this circle out too. To get uniform results, always use the same cutout plate as your template for marking other square boards. Cut all your plates.

Attach the plates for the stacked planter from top to bottom, ending with a solid base (a board with no cutout). To make this stacked planter, you need six pieces of 1 x 10 cedar. Stack the pieces on top of the base component, offsetting them slightly to create a spiral effect. Fasten the pieces together using glue and deck screws. Attach the pieces by driving the deck screws through the lower pieces into the upper pieces, fastening the base last.

Three-sided Stack

Use four plates on this option to create a planter with three cutout components and a solid base. Cut out a circle in three of the square boards as instructed on page 120. Measure and mark lines 1" from each side edge on the solid plate and one of the cutout components. Attach the inner plates with their inside faces flush with these lines. Fasten the solid plate to the sides with moisture-resistant glue and deck screws. Attach the remaining cutout plate to finish the planter. Insert a container, such as a painted coffee can.

"Chimney" Stack

Attach two plates with circular cutouts (see page 120) to the inside faces of two solid plates to make this planter. Measure and mark guidelines 2" from the top and bottom edges on the two solid plates. Fasten the two cutout plates between the others with moisture-resistant glue and deck screws, making sure their outside edges are flush with the drawn guidelines. Insert a container, such as a painted coffee can.

COFFEE TABLE PLANTER

At first glance this might look like an ambitious woodworking project, but in fact, this combination coffee table/ exterior planter is very easy to make with the most basic carpentry skills and tools you probably own already.

This planter functions as both a display for your potted plants and as an outdoor coffee table. It features a trough in the center that is designed to hold a 24" window-box style planter or up to three 8"-dia. pots. The table base is a simple frame made from dimension lumber that is available at any lumberyard. The only tools you need to build it are a saw, a framing square, and a drill/driver, and the sturdy frame can endure years of abuse from sun, rain, and snow.

TOOLS & MATERIALS

- 4 x 4" x 8-ft. exterior-rated wood (1)
- 2 x 8" x 8-ft. exterior-rated wood (3)
- 1 x 6" x 8-ft. exterior-rated wood (2)
- 1 x 4" x 8-ft. exterior-rated wood (1)
- 2" deck screws (1 lb.)
- 2½" deck screws (1 lb.)
- Saw
- Drill
- Countersink bit
- Sandpaper
- Clamps

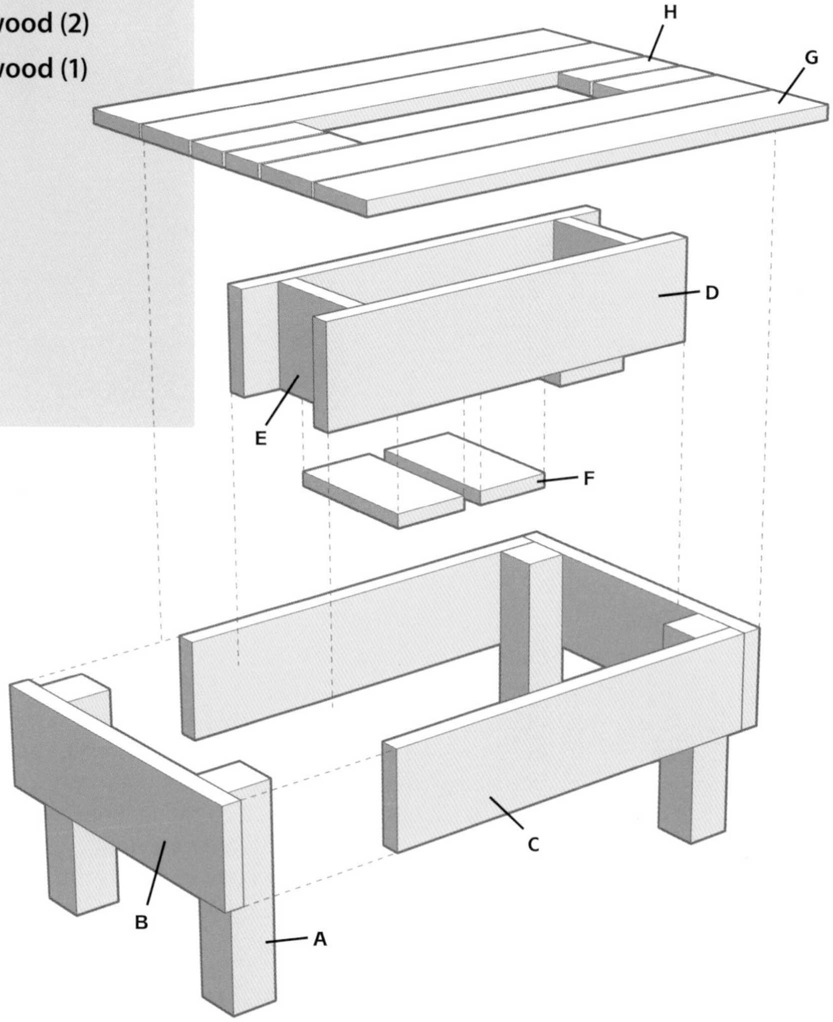

CUTTING LIST

KEY	PART	DIMENSION	PCS.	MATERIAL
A	Legs	3½ x 3½ x 16"	4	Exterior-rated wood
B	Short side rail	1½ x 7½ x 25½"	2	
C	Long side rail	1½ x 7½ x 33"	2	
D	Long cross supports	1½ x 7½ x 33"	2	
E	Short cross supports	1½ x 7½ x 8"	2	
F	Bottom supports	¾ x 5½ x 11"	3	
G	Wide top boards	¾ x 5½ x 41"	4	
H	Narrow top boards	¾ x 3½ x 8¾"	4	

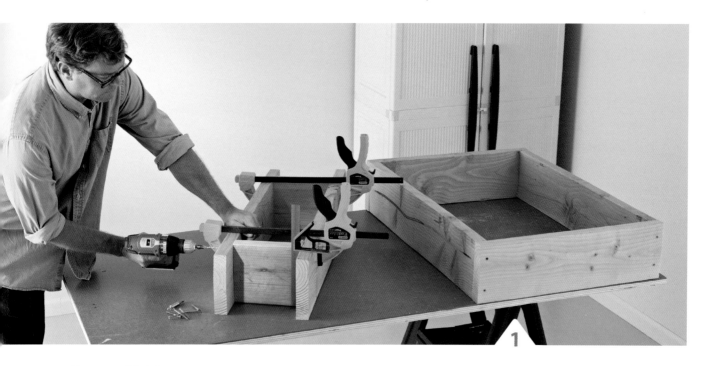

1

■ Assembly Tips

You can improve the appearance of your table with a few simple steps. First, take a few extra moments to line up the screws and space them evenly. Since most of the screws are exposed, having them look neat and symmetrical makes a big difference in how the finished piece looks. Also, countersink all exposed screws before driving the screws. The pilot holes will make it easier to fully drive the screws into the mating parts and help ensure that the pieces draw together to create a tight joint without splitting. When you drive a screw within 4" of the end of a board, there's always a chance the board will split, but if you predrill it won't happen.

■ A note about wood

Cedar and pressure-treated 2 x 8s and 1 x 6s have a tendency toward cupping, and trying to flatten cupped boards with screws or clamps will often just cause the wood to split. You can usually find flat pieces if you dig through the pile at the lumberyard. If you do have to use a cupped board for the top, put the cupped side down.

Make the wood frames. Use a miter saw or a circular saw to cut the base parts to length. If you are using a circular saw, clamp a straight edge to the work piece to help guide the saw as you cut. The short cross supports are spaced 24" apart, 3" from the ends of the long supports. Mark the locations of the short cross supports on the inside faces of the long cross supports. Then position the short cross supports on the marks and attach them to the long cross supports with two 2½" deck screws each. Center the cross supports on the short side rails and screw them in place, then attach the long side supports. Make sure you have the best sides of the boards facing out, and sand off any roughness or splintery edges. Assemble the frame upside down so you'll have a perfectly flat top

2 Finish the support frame by attaching the legs on the inside of the corners of the frame. Attach the legs to the side rails with 2½" deck screws. For a better appearance, space the screw locations evenly and symmetrically with a square. Also attach the bottom supports to the bottom of the long cross supports with predrilled 2" deck screws. The middle bottom support is positioned in the center of the long cross supports. Leave a 1½" space between the bottom supports.

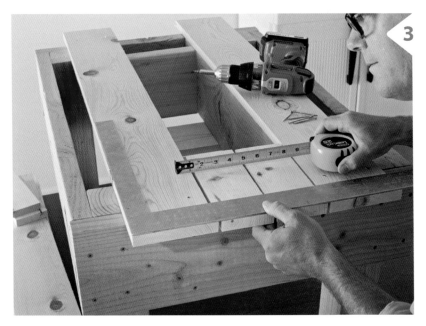

3 Cut all of the top boards to length. The top boards should overhang the frame by 2½" at the ends and 2¼ to 2½" on the sides (they can be moved in or out to equalize the spacing between boards). Position the wide top boards flush with the long inside edge of the planter support frame, then lay out all the other top boards first so you can check the spacing between boards, which should be about ¼". The long top boards can also overhang the trough slightly if the spacing between the short boards looks too wide. Attach the first top board alongside the planter frame with 2" exterior screws. Attach another wide top board along the opposite side of the planter frame. Then attach the remaining two wide top boards. Drive screws through the top boards and into the center of the side rails. Finally, center the narrow top boards between the wide top boards and attach them to the base frame with 2" deck screws.

Sand all the exposed wood and apply an exterior-rated finish, or leave the wood unfinished to weather naturally.

TRIPOD PLANTER

Three bent sticks bound together with a vine; planter projects don't get much easier to make than that.

This tripod was designed to hold a flowerpot, but it is such a versatile design that the possible uses are practically unlimited. If you are interested in learning the craft of creating furnishings with sticks, twigs, and branches, this very simple tripod is a great place to start. It is also a good way to use up the branches that you've collected that may be too twisted or oddly shaped for other bent branch projects. Remember that if you keep this planter outdoors where it will be exposed to the elements, the vine may need to be replaced after a year or two.

NOTE: The following bent branch planter projects are built using the same basic techniques featured in the Bent Branch Trellis chapter. Please see pages 56 to 59 for more helpful information on building with these materials.

1 Cut three sturdy legs to equal lengths, somewhat longer than the planned height of your planter—somewhere in the neighborhood of 32" is a good length. This next part is a bit tricky: Hold the poles in your non-dominant hand (your left hand if you're right-handed; right hand if you're left-handed), about 8" down from the top. Spread the poles out so the bottoms are equal distances from one another and the tops form a space into which you could place a flowerpot. (We will be enclosing this space, so you have to use your imagination here.) Drill pilot holes and attach each pole to the one on each side of it, using deck screws. Grip one pole in each hand and see if they move at all. If they do, add another screw or two at different angles. The tripod needs to be solid.

2 Wrap a flexible vine around the top of the tripod to create a bowl shape for a flowerpot to rest in. Use small nails or staples to secure the vine as you proceed. You can weave the vine in and out of itself if you wish—this produces an interesting texture.

EASEL PLANTER

For the more fanciful in spirit, this bent branch project really puts a focus on your favorite specimen plant.

Display your creativity and your favorite plants with this multi-dimensional garden project. Don't let the number of steps in the instructions for this project scare you, even if you don't have a lot of experience yet. Yes, there are quite a number of steps (especially if you're building the picture frame instead of using an old one), but they're all fairly simple and easy to do. When you finish building the easel, line the box with plastic and gravel and fill it with plants. The plants will look as though they are a framed picture. (Geraniums, lobelia, or wave petunias look lovely.) If you want to train a vine up the posts, you can plant it in either the box or in the ground beneath the easel.

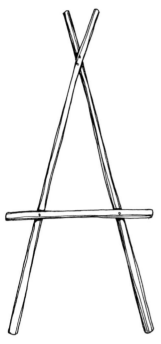

1 Take two of the 7-ft. easel legs and line up the thick ends with the edge of a worktable. The tops should cross, leaving a space at the top for the third piece to fit into later. Drill two pilot holes and screw the poles together at the top. Next, take the 32"-long brace and place it across the first two legs, about 36" from the bottom and centered across the legs. Drill pilot holes and drive a screw into each joint.

2 Stand the structure up, and lean the third 7-ft. leg into it at the top. Drill pilot holes and drive two screws to connect the third leg to each of the first two.

3 Run a 16" short brace from one front leg to the back, just below the 32" long brace, and parallel to the ground. Drill pilot holes and fasten the short brace in place with a screw at each joint. Repeat this process to add the second short brace, which completes the stand.

4 Cut three 1 x 4 cedar boards to 25" long. Set one of the boards flat on the work surface and another perpendicular to it. Secure the joint with three evenly spaced nails or screws. Repeat to add the other side to the box.

5 Measure the openings at the ends of the box; cut two pieces of cedar lumber to fit. Attach the ends to the box, driving nails or screws along each side and across the bottoms. Drill a few drainage holes in the floor of the box.

TOOLS & MATERIALS

- **Power drill**
- **Circular saw**
- **Legs: straight poles, 1" to 1½" in diameter, 6 ft. long (3)**
- **Long brace: 32" long (1)**
- **Short braces: straight sticks, 16" long (2)**
- **7 ft. of cedar 1 x 4**
- **An old picture frame or four pieces of 1 x 4 cedar lumber, 28 to 30"**
- **Nails and screws of the appropriate lengths**

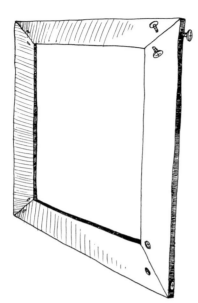

6 If you're making the picture frame, miter-cut each end of the 27" cedar 1 x 4s at a 45° angle. Lay the boards together in a square. At each corner, drive a screw in at an angle to join the two pieces. Then, close to the inside corner, drive a screw from the back of one piece, across the joint, and into the other (drill a pilot hole first). Add another screw going the opposite direction, about halfway along the joint. This can be tricky. Make sure you have not attached the frame to the table. Drive the final screw from the outside edge of one piece, through the joint and into the other.

7 Place the picture frame, face forward, onto the long brace of the easel. Drill pilot holes and drive screws in from the back in three places where the frame touches the poles. Put the box through the legs and rest it on the supports there. Attach the box to the supports with two screws on each side.

Resembling a hall table or sofa table, this lovely long planter is without question a fine example of garden furnishings.

TOOLS & MATERIALS

- Power drill
- Saw
- Hammer
- Pruning shears
- Staple gun
- Legs: straight poles, 36" long, 1½" to 2" in diameter (4)
- 10" crosspieces: straight branches, 1" in diameter (10)
- Shelf boards: (2) 1 × 4 and (2) 1 x 6, 32" long (4)
- Top rails: straight branches 1" in diameter, 34" to 36" long (2)
- Top trim: 34" straight pieces (2)
- Bottom trim: 32" straight pieces (2)
- Decorative branches
- Assorted nails, screws, and staples

HALL TABLE PLANTER

This project is much more than a simple planter; it is really more of a two-tier shelf for a container garden. Borrowing its form largely from tall, narrow tables typically found indoors, such as a hall table or a sofa table (the ones that go behind the sofa), it is long and lovely. When you choose plants for it, you might include some trailing or twining varieties, and then train the vines through and around the decorative branches.

This project does include a shelf. Rough-cut lumber typically looks best with this style, as opposed to the sanded-four-sides stock you'll find at the building center. True lumber yards will have rough lumber in random widths and lengths. Otherwise, use whatever you have on hand. Even in building centers you can usually find 1 x 6 or 1 x 8 cedar that is rough on one face. *(continued next page)*

HOW TO BUILD A HALL TABLE PLANTER

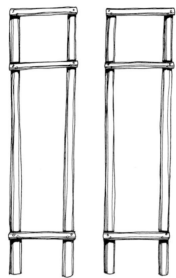

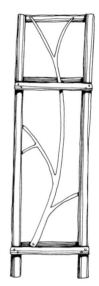

1 Arrange two 36" legs and two 10" crosspieces in a rough rectangle. Place the top crosspiece flush with the tops of the uprights and the bottom crosspiece about 4" above the ends. Add a third crosspiece 6 to 7" from the top. At each juncture, drill two pilot holes and drive a nail or screw into one hole of each pair. Adjust the framework until it's square, then add a second nail or screw at each juncture. Repeat this process to make a second frame.

2 Lay a leg frame on a worktable with the crosspieces facing down. Staple or nail interesting branches to each frame.

3 Put a 10" crosspiece across the frame, directly above the bottom crosspiece on the other side. Place the remaining 10" piece 7 to 8" down from the top. Drill pilot holes and drive screws to attach these crosspieces. These are your shelf supports.

4 Place two shelf boards between the two frames on the crosspieces at the bottom, and screw them into place, using two screws at the ends of each board to prevent warping. Repeat this process to add two boards to the upper crosspieces.

5 Tack a scrap of wood into place to square the structure. Add a top rail to the front and back, connecting the frames to one another at the top. Drill pilot holes and drive screws into each juncture. Add a strong branch to each side of the frame. Drill pilot holes and drive screws into each juncture.

6 Decorate the front and the back of the planter with branches and vines, creating triangular bracing in the process. You may even want to add decorations across the top. Remove the temporary brace you added in Step 5. Now, decorate the back. If your decoration pieces are flexible enough, loop them around one another, weave them through each other, or wrap them around the legs or top. If this is to be used indoors or on a porch protected from sun and rain, you might add other contrasting woods such as red dogwood or yellow willow.

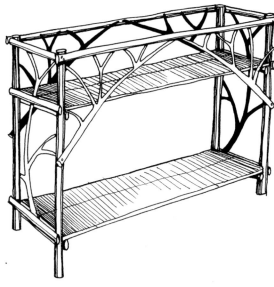

7 Place a 34-inch upper trim piece in front of the upper boards on each side. Drill pilot holes and attach the upper trim onto the legs. Put a 32" lower trim piece on the lower shelves. Attach it to the shelf boards.

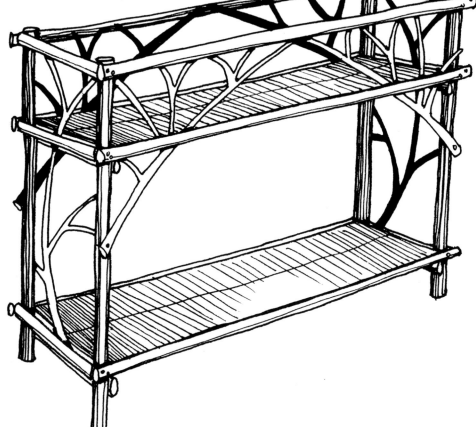

PLANTSTAND

This eye-catching plant stand looks more like fine furniture than a garden accessory. It is a good example of bent branch craftmanship.

TOOLS & MATERIALS

- ■ Power drill
- ■ Hammer
- ■ Saw
- ■ Pruning shears
- ■ Staple
- ■ Legs: 36" branches (4)
- ■ 10" rails (4)
- ■ 12" rails (4)
- ■ 14" rails (2)
- ■ Shelf slats: cut to fit (4 to 7)
- ■ Decorative branches
- ■ Assorted nails, screws, and staples

This small decorative plantstand can be built in a very short amount of time and makes a perfect accent to a deck or patio. Many people build a lot of these planters, scattering them about the garden as a unifying accent (that also happens to have a few hints of Mission furniture styling). And they can be moved around at will, letting you redecorate whenever you want. Because of the narrow footprint, you may have trouble with the planter wobbling, especially if it's placed on a hard-surface patio. If necessary, you can shear the bottoms of the legs until the planter rests solidly.

HOW TO BUILD A PLANTSTAND

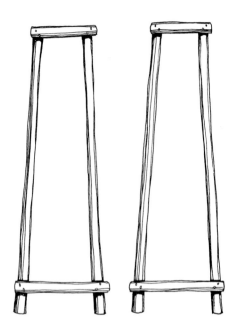

1 Place two 36" legs on a worktable; line up the ends with the edge of the table. Place a 10" top rail across the top, flush with the top of the legs. Drill two pilot holes at each juncture and drive one screw per joint. Place a 12" bottom rail about 4" from the ends of the poles; the brace should be parallel to the top piece and flush with the sides of the poles. Tack these joints also. Check to make sure the frame is lined up right (it's supposed to lean in a bit at the top). When you're satisfied, drive a second screw into each joint. Repeat this process to make a second frame.

2 Set the frames on the worktable with the rails facing down and the legs on top. Staple or nail branches to the frames in a design that pleases you. When you're finished, place a 10" rail across the two poles, about 6 to 7" down from the top.

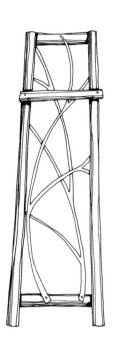

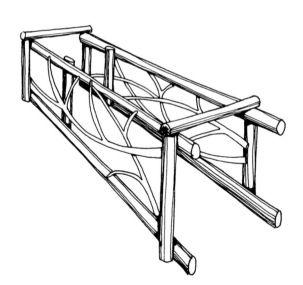

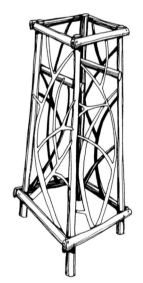

3 Join the two frames. Position a 12" rail between the tops of the frames and tack it. Add a 14" rail to join the frames near the bottom 12" rails. Flip the whole thing over and tack the other side.

4 Stand your frame up and adjust it until it's even and all four legs touch the ground. Once it's solid, drive a second screw into each joint on both sides of the planter. Decorate the two remaining sides from the inside. This may be a bit awkward.

5 With your planter standing up, cut short branches to span the rails that are 6 to 7" down from the top. Position the branches, drill pilot holes, and fasten the branches at both ends.

RAISED BEDS

If you've ever tried to grow plants in poor soil, you've probably discovered that it can be very frustrating unless you replace the bad soil with fresh, high quality topsoil—which means lots of back-breaking digging, often in dirt that seems like it's halfway to becoming solid rock. An easier solution is to ignore the existing soil and simply build a raised bed on top of it.

Raised beds have a lot to recommend them, but more than anything else, they're a great way to provide highly productive and well-drained soil for your plants, even if your yard is solid rock. With walls anywhere from 6 inches to 2 feet high, raised beds are usually built directly on top of the existing ground, separated from it (if at all) by a layer of newspaper or landscape fabric, although several inches of crushed gravel should be laid down first if the area is poorly drained.

Designs for raised beds can be as basic as a few boards arranged in a rectangle and joined at the corners, like the Raised Bed Kit on page 152 or the Utility Raised Bed on page 158. But they can also be more elaborate constructions that are as much garden feature as a place to grow veggies. The Backyard Bird Garden trellis (page 140) and the Half-Lap Planter (page 165) are two examples.

Another advantage of raised beds is that most can also be modified for more productive growing by adding either lightweight plastic covers to control heat loss and protect against early frosts, or netting to keep deer and raccoons from eating the crop (see Raised Planting Bed and Cover, page 146, for an example). They can even be raised off the ground, making gardening easier for those with bad backs and knees and also keeping tasty veggies out of the reach of slugs and other garden pests (see the Lettuce Table page 154).

It's best to fill raised beds with fresh soil from a garden supplier or home center. Special soil mixes for planters are available and do a great job of nourishing young plants, but standard, sterilized topsoil also works well. Avoid using topsoil scraped from your yard or a nearby field; it's almost always contaminated with weed seeds and may not be right for what you want to grow. If you want to mix your own, you can find a number of different recipes on the Internet. One commonly used formula is equal parts peat moss, compost, and vermiculite.

Most raised beds can be made with basic tools and minimal carpentry skills. If you own and can use a saw, a drill, and a few standard hand tools, you can make your own high-yielding raised bed in a few hours, for as little as $50 to $75, and start growing your own vegetables or garden-show quality flowers the next day.

TIMBER RAISED BED

The most basic raised planting bed is simply made from landscape timbers with staggered end joints. This one is lined with landscape fabric.

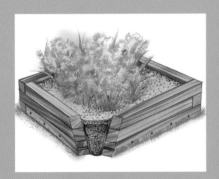

Raised garden beds are easy to weed, simple to water, and the soil quality is easier to control, ensuring that your plants thrive. Your garden beds can be built at any height up to waist-level. It's best not to build them much taller than that, however, to make sure you can reach the center of your bed. This basic but very sturdy raised bed is made with 4 × 4 landscape timbers stacked with their ends staggered in classic log-cabin style. The corners are pinned together with 6" galvanized spikes (or, you can use timber screws). It is lined with landscape fabric and includes several weep holes in the bottom course for drainage. Consider adding a 2 × 8 ledge on the top row (see the large red bed on page 137). Corner finials (also on page 137) improve the appearance and provide hose guides to protect the plants in the bed.

TIP: For low-growing plants, position the bed with a north-south orientation, so both sides of the bed will be exposed to direct sunlight. For taller plants, position the bed east-west.

HOW TO BUILD A TIMBER RAISED BED

TOOLS & MATERIALS

- **Reciprocating saw**
- **Drill with ³⁄₁₆, ½" bits**
- **Stakes and string**
- **4 x 4" x 8 ft. landscape timbers (4)**
- **6" galvanized landscape spikes**
- **Landscape fabric**
- **Roofing nails**

Outline a 3 × 5-ft. area with stakes and mason's string. Remove all grass inside the area, then dig a 2"-deep × 6"-wide trench along the inside perimeter of the outline. Cut each of the four timbers into one 54" piece and one 30" piece, using a reciprocating saw or circular saw.

Set the first course of timbers in the trench. Check the timbers for level along their lengths and at the corners, adding or removing soil to adjust, as needed. Position the second course on top of the first, staggering the corner joints with those in the first course. Fasten the courses together at each corner with pairs of 6" nails driven through ³⁄₁₆" pilot holes.

Line the bed with landscape fabric to contain the soil and help keep weeds out of the bed. Tack the fabric to the lower part of the top course with roofing nails. Some gardeners recommend drilling 1"-dia. weep holes in the bottom timber course at 2-ft. intervals. Fill with a blend of soil, peat moss, and fertilizer (if desired) to within 2 or 3" of the top.

This all-in-one raised bed project has a built-in wood trellis structure for your favorite climbing plants, plus a post-mounted birdhouse to help attract birds to your yard.

BACKYARD BIRD GARDEN

This project combines a raised bed with a trellis, allowing you to plant a mixture of ground plants or vegetables and climbing plants in a small, compact space. The trellis incorporates a few additional features like a birdhouse and extended crosspieces for hanging bird feeders, wind chimes, seasonal or indoor plants, or anything else that you would like to display. It was designed mostly for small yards or patios, for urban gardens where space is at a premium, even for apartment terraces—but it can be used anywhere, no matter how big your garden is. The basic idea behind it was to create a sort of outdoor terrarium, a densely-planted environment that would attract birds and pollinating insects.

This design is meant to be placed directly on the ground, but it can be adapted to a deck or patio by nailing 1x slats to the bottom and covering them with aluminum screen or landscape fabric to keep the dirt in.

TOOLS & MATERIALS

- ☐ 2 x 10" x 8-ft, cedar (2)
- ☐ 2 x 4" x 8-ft. cedar (4)
- ☐ 2 x 2" x 8-ft. cedar (5)
- ☐ 2½" deck screws (1 lb.)
- ☐ 1⅝" deck screws (1 lb.)
- ☐ Hemp garden twine or rope
- ☐ Birdhouse (optional)
- ☐ Saw
- ☐ Drill
- ☐ Countersink bit
- ☐ Clamps
- ☐ Framing square

CUTTING LIST

PART	DIMENSION	PCS.	MATERIAL
Long side	2 x 10 x 48"	2	Cedar
Short side	2 x 10 x 30"	2	
Post	2 x 4" x 6 ft.	3	
Long post	2 x 4 x 8 ft. *	1	
Corner support	2 x 4 x 8¼"	2	
Front/rear crosspiece	2 x 2 x 27"	4	
Side crosspiece	2 x 2 x 25¾"	5	
Front/rear hanger	2 x 2 x 37"	2	
Side hanger	2 x 2 x 35¾"	1	

* If you chose not to attach a birdhouse, cut this six feet long instead of eight. The extra length of the 2 x 2 hangers is also optional.

HOW TO BUILD A BACKYARD BIRD GARDEN

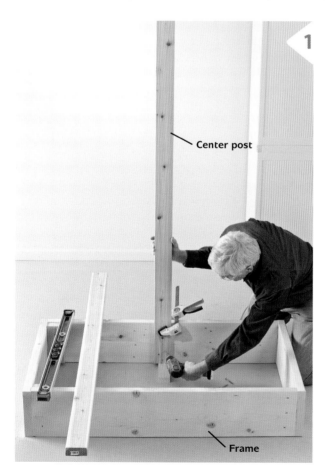

1

Center post

Frame

To build this backyard bird garden structure, start by cutting the parts to the sizes listed above and assembling the frame with deck screws. Be sure to drill pilot holes. Cedar was used so that edibles could be planted, but if you're not planting veggies, less-expensive pressure-treated wood is fine. Square the frame and set the posts at the centers and in the corners and screw them in with several 2½" deck screws. Make sure the center posts are parallel with the corner posts. Put the 8-ft. post in at one of the corners. If you don't want a birdhouse on top of the post, just cut it to the same length as the other posts. Also install a short piece of 2 x 4 at each front corner to strengthen the joints. To prevent the post ends from wicking up moisture and rotting prematurely, slip a spacer under the posts before attaching them. When the raised bed is done, before the soil goes in, pile some gravel under and around the posts and they'll stay drier. This gap will also make it easier to fasten slats on underneath if you want to set the project on a deck or patio.

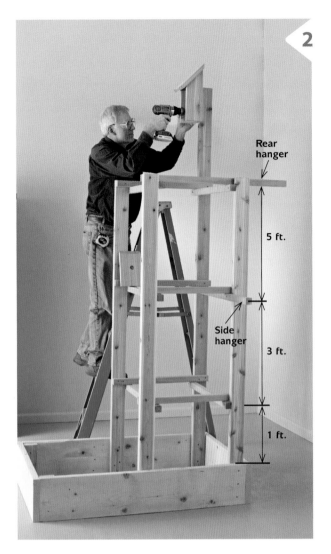

2

Install the 2 x 2 crosspieces and accessories. Mark the bottoms of the front and back 2 x 2 crosspieces at 1 ft., 3 ft., and 5 ft. up from the 2 x 10. Predrill the 2 x 2s, then screw them in place. Add the side 2 x 2s on top of the front and back crosspieces. If you would like to hang plants or a bird feeder, substitute the long 2 x 2s for a few of the regular size ones. Here, a small cedar birdhouse is being attached at the top of an extra-tall corner post. You can purchase these at most craft stores and birding stores, or you can make a simple one yourself with cut-off lumber.

3

After all the 2 x 2s are fastened on the frame, add hemp or jute twine or rope for the climbing plants. You can start from screws or nails attached to the inside of the frame, as shown in this plan, or just string the twine across the 2 x 2s—either way, it will quickly be covered by climbing plants.

HOW TO BUILD A BIRDHOUSE

The birdhouse shown here is pretty much as simple as a birdhouse can get. To make it, you'll need about 3 feet of 1 x 4 (we used cedar here), about 2 feet of 1 x 6 and about a foot of 1 x 8. Make a box that's 12¾" tall and has 1 x 4 sides and 1 x 6 front and back. On the front, measure up 8" and make a mark. Draw diagonal cutting lines on the sides from the 8" mark to the top of the back. Carefully cut along the lines with a handsaw to remove the top of the box. Make a 3½ x 3½" floor from a piece of 1 x 4 and install it in the box bottom. Drill a 1"-dia. hole in the front wall. The centerpoint of the hole should be about 3" down from the top of the box front. Cut a piece of 1 x 8 to 8½" long. If you want to get fancy you can make bevel cuts that have the same angle as the sloping box sides—these are called plumb cuts. Attach the top so the back edge is flush with the back of the box. To make it easier to hang the birdhouse, temporarily remove the front, then drive screws through the inside of the back wall and into the mounting (see step 2, above). Reattach the front.

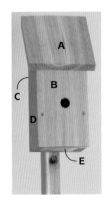

CUTTING LIST

KEY	PART	SIZE	MATERIAL
A	**Top**	¾ x 7¼ x 8½"	1 x 8 cedar
B	**Front**	¾ x 5½ x 8"	1 x 6 cedar
C	**Back**	¾ x 5½ x 12¾"	1 x 6 cedar
D	**Side (2)**	¾ x 3½ x 12¾"	1 x 4 cedar
E	**Floor**	¾ x 3½ x 3½"	1 x 4 cedar

RAISED BED
PYRAMID

This raised bed is made from 4 x 4s posts and features simple
construction and distinctive design. We built this one 4-ft. square,
but this design can be made bigger or smaller, with more or fewer
levels—as long as it's square. With four different levels and thirteen
sections, there are almost unlimited possibilities for dramatic combinations
of plants and colors. In addition, although all the plants grow in the
same soil, the 4 x 4s that define the sections make it easier to keep more
aggressive plants under control and to establish separate growing areas.

A little heavy lifting (not that
heavy really) and some timber
screws are all you really need to
make this interesting, pyramid-
shaped raised bed.

TOOLS & MATERIALS

- ☐ 4 x 4" x 8-ft. (7)
- ☐ 5" or 6" self drilling, exterior-grade lag screws (40) (GRK and TimberLok are two common brands)
- ☐ Miter saw or circular saw
- ☐ Drill or impact driver
- ☐ Tape measure

CUTTING LIST

PART	DIMENSION	PCS.	MATERIAL
Base	44½"	8	Rot-resistant wood
First level	30½"	4	Rot-resistant wood
Second level	20½"	4	Rot-resistant wood
Third level	13 ⅜"	4	Rot-resistant wood

HOW TO MAKE A RAISED BED PYRAMID

1

Cut the 4 x 4 parts to length and assemble the large square base. Some circular saws and some miter saws (all 10" and 12" cut in one pass) do not have enough cutting capacity to manage a 4 x 4, so you'll have to carefully make one cut and then flip it and cut from the opposite side. All the pieces for the base are cut the same size and joined end to end, with the second layer overlapping the first. As you can see from the photos, the way the pieces go together is a little different than standard construction for a square box, which typically uses two long and two shorter pieces, but it's just as sturdy, and you can just set up a stop block or a jig for each level and cut all the pieces exactly the same size. You just have to remember how the pieces are going together, because it's easy to lose track as you move from level to level.

After the two base levels are screwed together, mark the centerpoints on each outside edge. Measure diagonally from centerpoint to centerpoint, subtract 3½" for the thickness of the adjoining piece, and cut four pieces to that size. Join them together just as you did the first level, with the end of each piece fastened to the beginning of the next piece. The outside corners of the square should sit at the center mark you made earlier. Repeat the same steps for each additional level. The four diagonal measurements at each level should be close to the same; if not, the lower box is out of square or the wood is warped. The simplest solution is to just adjust it until you're satisfied with it visually and then cut the 4 x 4s to the average of the measurements and split the difference when you place the box on the lower frame. If you have to cut a level smaller, cut the identical amount from all sides so the box stays square—or you'll run into the same problem with the next level.

Build and install the third level, using the centerpoints for alignment. Use self-drilling, galvanized fasteners, if you can find them, for these and all other joints. They're a bit more expensive, but they're stronger than traditional lag screws and save a lot of assembly time, since even large bolts can be driven in by a drill equipped with a nut driver or Torx bit without predrilling. Use two per corner—one horizontal and one vertical, with an extra bolt in the middle of the second base layer. You can also use traditional lag screws or 6" spikes, but predrill to avoid splitting the wood.

Complete the construction and apply your finish as desired. Exterior wood stain with UV protectant is a good choice for a project like this—the version seen here is made of Douglas fir, which should have a protective finish. Set the raised bed in place and shim it level with dirt or gravel. If the ground is uneven, cut out the turf and drop the raised bed in. If you're on a slope, you can add a 2 x 4 or 4 x 4 on the low end or dig the high end into the ground. Spread out landscape fabric around the bottom to stop grass and weeds from growing through. Fill the raised bed with topsoil, cover the bare dirt with wood mulch, and then start planting.

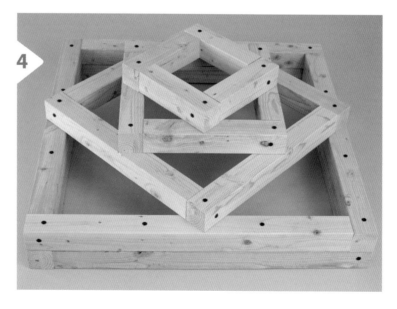

RAISED PLANTING BED & COVER

Filled with carefully prepared soil, a raised bed offers high yields in a relatively small space. This simple, inexpensive bed design includes wood cleats installed along its top edges—a handy feature for clamping down covers of all types.

A raised bed is much like a container garden in that it offers total control over the soil content and quality, without the worry of compaction from walking through the garden. Containment of the soil also prevents erosion, helps with weed encroachment, and improves water drainage. For many urban gardeners, a raised bed is the best—and often only—way to grow vegetables and other crop plants in tight spaces.

Another advantage of a raised bed is that the frame around the bed provides a structure for adding covers to protect plants from cold, wind, and snow, or to erect netting to keep out pests. The simple cover frame shown here is much like a hoophouse structure used by farmers to shelter rows of crops on a temporary basis. Ours is made with PVC pipe and is easy to disassemble for storage at the end of the season. The lightweight frame is perfect for a canopy of plastic sheeting (for warmth in colder weather), spun fleece (for insect protection), or deer netting.

The raised bed frame is made with a single course of 2 × 10 lumber. You can use smaller lumber for a shallower bed, or go higher with more courses and taller corner posts. Unless your bed will be used strictly for ornamental plants (not food), don't use pressure-treated lumber, due to the risk of chemical contamination. Instead, choose a naturally decay-resistant species such as all-heart redwood, cedar, cypress, or Douglas fir.

TOOLS & MATERIALS

- Tape measure
- Hammer
- Circular saw
- Square
- Hand sledge
- Level
- Spring clamps (12)

- Hacksaw or pipe cutter
- 3½" and 1¼" deck screws
- 10-ft. 2 × 10 (2)
- 8-ft. 2 × 10 (1)
- 8-ft. 4 × 4 (1)
- 8-ft. 2 × 4 (1)
- 8-ft. 1 × 4 (1)

- Reciprocating saw or handsaw
- Permanent marker
- Drill and countersink bit and ³⁄₁₆" twist bit
- ¾"-dia. × 10 ft. PVC pipe (7)
- 1¾" #8 stainless steel machine bolts and wing nuts (6)
- Cover material (8 × 14 ft.)

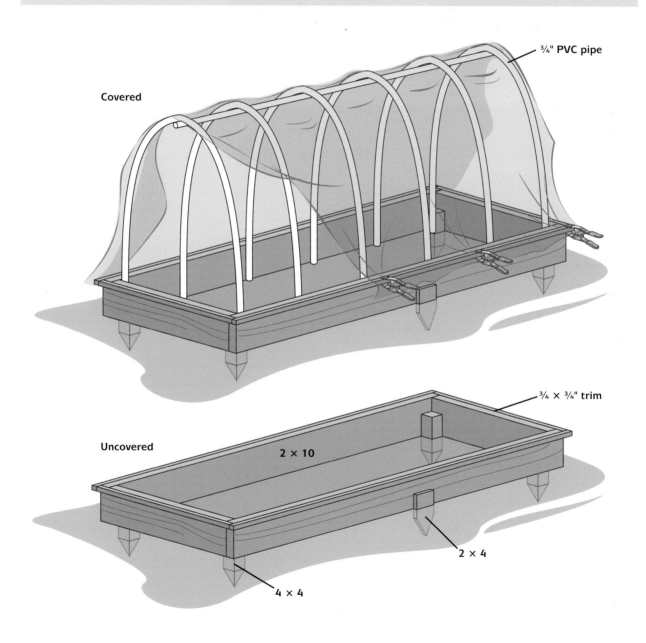

¾" PVC pipe

Covered

¾ × ¾" trim

Uncovered

2 × 10

2 × 4

4 × 4

HOW TO BUILD A RAISED BED WITH COVER

1 Cut the two frame ends to length (45") from an 8-ft. 2 × 10, using a circular saw and a square or straightedge to ensure straight cuts. For the frame side pieces, trim the ends of the 10-ft. 2 × 10s, if necessary, so they are square and measure 120".

2 Assemble the frame by setting the sides over the ends of the end pieces so they are flush at the top and outside edges. Drill three evenly spaced pilot holes through the sides and into the end pieces and fasten the parts with 3½" deck screws.

3 Create the corner posts by cutting the 8-ft. 4 × 4 into four pieces roughly 24" each. Trim the ends of each post to a point, using a reciprocating saw or handsaw.

4 Set the bed frame into place, then measure diagonally between opposing corners to check for square: the frame is square when the measurements are equal. Tip: For general soil preparation, turn over the soil beneath the bed and add compost or manure, as desired, before setting down the frame.

5 Drive a post at each corner inside the frame, using a hand sledge and a wood block to prevent mushrooming the post top. Drive the posts until the tops are about 2" below the top of the bed frame. Check the frame for level, then drill pilot holes and fasten each side and end piece to a post with 3½" deck screws.

6 Add a 2 × 4 stake at the midpoint of each frame side, to help keep the lumber from bowing out over time. Cut the stake to a point and drive it down below the top edge of the frame. Tack the stake to the frame with a couple of screws.

7 Install the cleats: Rip a 1 × 4 into four ¾"-wide strips, using a circular saw or table saw (it's okay if the last strip isn't exactly ¾"). Fasten the strips along the perimeter of the bed frame, flush with the top edges, using 1¼" deck screws driven through pilot holes. Cut the strips to length as needed to complete each run. Fill the bed with soil and compost, as desired.

8 Mark and drill the ridge pole for the cover frame, using one of the 10-ft. PVC pipes. Make a mark 1" from each end, then mark every 24" in between. The marks should form a straight line down the length of the pipe. At each mark, drill a ³⁄₁₆"-dia. hole straight down through the pipe.

9 Prepare the cover frame ribs by cutting six ¾"-dia. PVC pipes to length at 96", using a hacksaw or tubing cutter. Then, make a mark at the midpoint (48") of each rib, and drill a ³⁄₁₆"-dia. hole straight through the pipe at each mark.

10 Assemble the cover frame, using 1¾" machine bolts and wing nuts. Fit a rib over the top of the ridge pole at each hole location. Insert the bolt through the rib and ridge and secure with a wing nut. The wing nuts allow for quick disassembly of the frame.

11 Install the cover frame into the bed by fitting one end of each rib against a frame side, inside the box area, and then bending the rib and fitting the other end inside the frame. It helps to have two people for this job, starting at one end of the frame and working down.

12 Add the cover material of your choice. Drape the cover over the cover frame, center it side-to-side and end-to-end, and secure it on all sides with clamps fitted over the cleats. To prevent overheating with plastic covers, you can roll up the cover at the ends and clamp it to the outside ribs.

RAISED BED KITS

Raised bed kits are very popular right now, as they are easy to set up and have become available in a much greater assortment of sizes and styles. The composite model above, made by Greenland Gardeners (see Resources, page 169), is actually one fourth of the larger kit seen on the next page. Modular kits like these can be added onto and reconfigured in many ways.

A raised bed kit is a great way to get a raised bed garden started in an hour or less. Raised garden bed kits come in many styles. One popular type has composite panels with notched ends that simply slide into grooved connectors. It's available in several different-sized kits that can be assembled into various-sized boxes, or, with a few extra boards and accessories, made into large configurations with multiple growing areas, or even stacked to increase bed height.

Find a flat area of the yard or garden. Check the position of the sun to make sure your raised bed will get sufficient sunlight during the course of the day. If everything looks good, assemble the panels and corner brackets. The

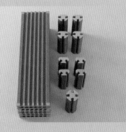

The Raised Bed Kit can be assembled in a number of different configurations using standard composite planks and three types of locking connectors.

panels have grooved, T-shaped ends that slide easily into matching pockets in the corners, and the corners align the boards perpendicular to each other. After the kit is assembled in its final position, cut into the ground around the edges of the planting bed box with a square-nose spade, move the box, and then slice off the sod in the bed area. You can also just leave the sod and cover the ground with several layers of newspaper or a layer of landscape fabric, but if the site is at all uneven removing the sod will make it

easier to level the bed. Either way, cover the ground with a weed blocker of newspaper or fabric so weeds and grass won't grow through. Finally, shovel in the dirt and start planting. That's all there is to it.

For a larger or more elaborate raised bed with multiple growing areas or a different shape, use extra panels and additional connectors. The 3-way and 4-way connectors combined with corner connectors create a number of different options for divided beds, rectangles, L-shapes, T-shapes, and others.

HOW TO ASSEMBLE A WOOD KIT

1

2

Some have modular plastic or composite panels that fit together with grooves or with hardware. Others feature wood panels and metal corner hardware. Most kits can be stacked to increase bed height.

On a flat surface, assemble the panels and corner brackets (or hinge brackets) using the included hardware. Follow the kit instructions, making sure all corners are square.

3

4

Set the box down, experimenting with exact positioning until you find just the spot and angle you like. Be sure to observe the sun over an entire day when choosing the sunniest spot you can for growing vegetables. Cut into the ground around the edges of the planting bed box with a square-nose spade, move the box, and then slice off the sod in the bed area.

Set the bed box onto the installation site and check it for level. Add or remove soil as needed until it is level. Stake the box to the ground with the provided hardware. Add additional box kits on top of or next to the first box. Follow the manufacturer's suggestion for connecting the modular units. Line the bed or beds with landscape fabric and fill with soil to within 2" or so of the top box.

LETTUCE TABLE

The lettuce table can be used to grow more than lettuce. It simply draws its name from its original purpose, which is to provide a shallow bed for growing lettuces in an easy-to-reach spot that can be moved easily around your yard. This interpretation is on the large side to allow you to grow several varieties, but you can easily modify the simple plan to build a more compact version.

The lettuce table solves a number of gardening problems that home gardeners confront when growing tasty vegetables and herbs. First, and most important, it moves the crop up and out of the way of rabbits, slugs, and other destructive pests. Second, it's portable, so it can be moved to follow or avoid the sun, or brought into the garage on frosty nights. Third, it can be set up on convenient but barren spots like decks, patios and driveways. Fourth, it allows you to garden at a comfortable height, saving wear and tear on knees and backs. Fifth, you can easily replace the growing media every year and precisely control moisture and fertilizer, giving you better, more predictable yields. And finally, it provides accessible gardening for those in wheelchairs.

The frame of this lettuce table, which will be in contact with the soil, can be made from cedar, redwood, or any other naturally rot-resistant wood. It is left unfinished on the inside. Pressure-treated wood is used for the rest of the framework because it's less expensive and will resist decay for decades. The galvanized hardware cloth across the bottom is an inexpensive way to support the weight of the soil; you can substitute cedar boards, galvanized metal flashing, or any other rot-resistant, nontoxic material that can hold the weight. No matter what you use to hold the weight, the soil is held in place with heavy-duty landscape fabric or aluminum screen mesh.

TOOLS & MATERIALS

- [ ] 2 x 4" x 8-ft. cedar (1)
- [ ] 2 x 4" x 12-ft. cedar (1)
- [ ] 2 x 4" x 8-ft. pressure-treated (1)
- [ ] 2 x 4" x 12-ft. pressure-treated (3)
- [ ] 1 x 2" x 8-ft. pressure-treated (3)
- [ ] ¼" galvanized hardware cloth
- [ ] Stapler with ⁵⁄₁₆" stainless steel staples
- [ ] Landscape fabric
- [ ] Construction adhesive
- [ ] 2½" deck screws (1 lb.)
- [ ] 1" roofing nails (1 lb.)
- [ ] Countersink bit
- [ ] Framing square
- [ ] Leather gloves
- [ ] Drill
- [ ] Miter saw
- [ ] Tin snips
- [ ] Hammer
- [ ] Caulk gun
- [ ] Clamps

CUTTING LIST

PART	DIMENSION	PCS.	MATERIAL
Tray side	2 x 4 x 72"	2	Cedar
Tray ends and divider	2 x 4 x 21"	3	Cedar
Outer leg	2 x 4 x 36"	4	Pressure-treated
Inner leg	2 x 4 x 20½"	4	Pressure-treated
Bottom leg	2 x 4 x 8½"	4	Pressure-treated
Stretcher	2 x 4 x 69"	1	Pressure-treated
Top stretcher	2 x 4 x 72"	1	Pressure-treated
Center support	2 x 4 x 19"	1	Pressure-treated
Side rail	2 x 4 x 24"	2	Pressure-treated
Side trim	1 x 2 x 71"	2	Pressure-treated
End trim	1 x 2 x 17"	2	Pressure-treated

HOW TO BUILD A LETTUCE TABLE

1. Cut the parts for the table frame to length and assemble the cedar top tray with the center divider. Predrill all screw holes to avoid splits, and use two screws at each corner. Use 2½" (or 3") deck screws. This design is for a 2 x 6 ft. tray, but you can make it larger or smaller.

Wearing leather gloves, cut the hardware cloth to size. Cut out a 2 x 4" section at each corner for the legs. Center it on the underside of the cedar frame—it should be about ¼" in from the edge on all sides. Nail it every 6" on the center divider, but first mark and cut out a 2 x 4" slot at the center of the divider. Pull the cloth flat and nail it several times on each side and the ends. No need to overdo it—the edges of the cloth will be covered and secured with 1 x 2s later.

Cut the legs from the pressure-treated wood and assemble them into two leg pairs. Screw the inner and outer legs together, leaving a 3½" gap at the top. The top frame will sit on the ledges created at the top. Leave the bottom legs off for now. Make sure the legs are parallel to each other, then join them together with the side rails. Spread a bead of construction adhesive before attaching the two pieces. Set the legs down parallel to each other and join them with the side rails.

With the tray turned upside down, fit the legs onto the ends. Check that they're square to the frame and sitting flat underneath it—if you see daylight between the inner leg and the tray, trim the outer leg a little so the gap disappears. Screw each leg to both parts of the cedar frame.

Attach the stretcher with 2½" screws. Use clamps to hold the wood in place while you predrill and fasten. Also measure and cut the bottoms of the legs, and fasten with adhesive and screws.

6

7

Place the tray on the ground, right-side up. Screw the top stretcher to the rails and lower stretcher. Measure the distance from the stretchers to the center divider and cut and fasten the support. Add 1/16" to your measurement just to make sure you have a snug fit.

Predrill the 1 x 2s every 8 to 10". Flip the tray over then screw the 1 x 2s to the bottom of the tray, flush with the outside edges and covering the hardware cloth.

8

Finally, staple on landscape fabric or aluminum screen on the inside of the tray to hold the soil in. Fill the tray with a soilless growing media and fertilizer—not ordinary topsoil. For best results, replace the soilless mix every year, as it becomes compressed over time.

UTILITY RAISED BED

About as simple as a large raised bed can get, this project is designed to take a lot of dirt and support a lot of plants. It is simple 2 x 6 construction, but because of its size it should be reinforced in the center with a tie rod or cable to keep the sides from bowing out.

This raised bed is designed to be an easy-to-build utilitarian growing space for intensive growing of vegetable crops, and although it's very appealing when it's full of growing plants it's not really intended to be a decorative garden showpiece. The walls are made from three stacked 2 x 6s, though you can build it higher by using 2 x 8s instead of 2 x 6s. For extra strength the corners interlock, and are also fastened to vertical 2 x 6 braces hidden inside the wall that hold the boards together. More vertical 2 x 6 braces are also attached on the inside every 4 or 5 ft. to hold the 2 x 6 planks together. For long planters galvanized tie rods are used every 5 to 8 ft. to connect the opposing walls and keep them from spreading apart. If you don't like the idea of tie rods, you can build a dividing wall from 2 x 6s to hold the sides together.

Make the walls of the raised bed from cedar, redwood, or other naturally rot-resistant wood, or even from composite lumber, though you'll have to double the number of tie rods or dividing walls to keep the flexible composite boards from bowing out. If you're not going to be planting vegetables, you can build the raised bed from pressure-treated wood.

TOOLS & MATERIALS

- [ ] **2 x 6" x 16-ft. cedar (8), (for project as built in photo)**
- [ ] **2 x 6" x 8-ft. (1) (for braces)**
- [ ] **6 ft. x ½" galvanized tie rods (4), with washers and bolts**
- [ ] **2½" deck screws (5 lb.)**
- [ ] **Circular saw or sliding miter saw**
- [ ] **Crushed gravel (as needed)**

- [ ] **Countersink bit**
- [ ] **Drill**
- [ ] **Wrench**
- [ ] **½" spade bit**
- [ ] **Shovel**

▨ Siting Your Planter

You can set the planter directly on the ground if your soil is reasonably well-drained. If your soil is clay or drainage is a problem, spread several inches of crushed gravel on the ground so that excess water can drain away, and set the bed on the gravel. This will also keep the base of the raised bed from rotting. Either way, spread a layer of newspaper over the ground before you add soil to smother any weeds. Level the bed, if needed, by eye. If it looks off balance or twisted or low at one end, add gravel under the low spots to lift the frame up.

CUTTING LIST

KEY	PART	DIMENSION	PCS.	MATERIAL
A	Side	2 x 6" x 16 ft.	6	Cedar
B	End	2 x 6" x 5 ft.	6	Cedar
C	Braces	2 x 6 x 15"	12	Cedar

VARIATIONS

ABOVE: This basic raised bed is constructed from two 2 x 8s per side, and has a center divider holding the two sides together instead of rebar.

RIGHT: Another type of basic raised bed. This design uses metal angles to hold the corners together, along with heavy metal stakes at the sides to resist spreading and movement.

1 Start by screwing together the first level, predrilling the holes with a countersink bit so you don't split the ends. After the first level is done, attach vertical 2 x 6s at the inside corners. Add the next layer of 2 x 6s, alternating the lengths to make the corner a little tighter and more interesting-looking. The sides and ends are all equal lengths, so adjoining corners are alternated in opposite ways, and the overall size of the raised bed is 16 ft., 1½" x 5 ft., 1½". Attach more vertical 2 x 6 braces every 4 ft. or 5 ft. on the inside of the 2 x 6s.

2 A long raised bed of 2 x 6s needs to be held together at the center or it will bulge out from the weight of the dirt. Add a 2 x 6 vertical support and drill two ½"-dia. holes at the same points on both sides. Push galvanized, threaded tie rods through the holes, then thread galvanized washers and nuts over the ends and tighten until the distance at the center and the ends is the same. Threaded tie rods are zinc-plated rods, usually ⅜, ½, or ⅝" in diameter, that are tapped with threads over the entire length. If gaps eventually appear at the corners, dig out some of the adjoining soil to reduce the pressure, push the walls back together as best you can, and reinforce the corners with large metal angles. Move your bed to its site (unless you built it on site, which is a good idea when you can do it). Finally, spread newspaper over the ground to kill off any weeds, then fill with high-quality soil and start growing your crops.

Tip: Trim off any protruding hardware.

RAISED BED ROCK GARDEN

This is a simple, very attractive, and generally permanent raised bed that can be built in almost any shape or size, and is usually about 1 ft. to 2 ft. high. The challenge of a raised bed rock garden is selecting and stacking the rocks and blending them into the terrain so that instead of a random, raw-looking pile of rocks, you see a collection of rocks full of contrast and detail that look like they've been there forever.

If you don't have a rocky field or stream nearby, you can find a wide variety of rock at any stone yard and most garden supply stores. Rock can be surprisingly expensive—from $200 to $600 a ton or more, depending on the type, the source, whether it's cut, cost of delivery, and other factors. Multiply the lineal feet you'll need by the approximate height of the wall, then by the thickness, so you can get a realistic idea of cost. Stone is sold by weight, but suppliers will translate cubic feet into

A raised bed made from rocks can be anything from a formal rock wall to a gently sloped collection of field stone planted with herbs and small flowers. Either type will last forever.

weight. Cubic feet are obtained by multiplying length x width x height; a cubic yard is 27 cubic feet, or 3 ft. x 3 ft. x 3 ft.

If you're getting a small order and hauling the rock yourself in a truck or trailer, most suppliers will let you pick your own, but even if they just dump a truckload in your yard you'll find plenty of variety. If possible, buy a mix of sizes—it will make the wall look more interesting and make it easier to avoid large gaps.

There are three basic options for a raised bed rock garden. The first is to simply build up a pile of topsoil, slope it 30° or so, embed rocks in the sides and fill it all with plants. The next option is to build a tighter rock wall at a 30 to 60° angle, with a wider base for stability, but still pitched back against the dirt it's enclosing. The third option is to build a thicker, more traditional vertical wall with a tamped gravel base several inches thick.

Rocks can just be set on the ground, but unless you're going with the simplest option, it's better to start the bottom course in a shallow trench. Partially buried, the rocks will look more natural, like they've been there forever. They'll also stay in place better when the ground freezes. It also makes it easier to hide the bottom edge of the landscape fabric, if you choose to use it. If you're building the wall on a sloping site, you'll need to excavate a foot or so of existing soil to make room for topsoil.

If you want to keep the rock wall unplanted, landscape fabric can help keep unwanted weeds and grasses from getting established between the rocks. A good strategy is to place fabric out to the edge of the bottom course, then bring it up the backside of the rock, holding it in place with the soil. You can pack soil into crevices between the rocks as you plant them, so that desirable plants get established and crowd out weeds that try to take root. Inside the raised bed, place sheets of newspaper over the ground instead of landscape fabric to kill off any existing growth without blocking out beneficial earthworms.

The easiest way to make a sloping rock wall is to dump a load of soil in the desired location and then shape it and build up the rocks against it, packing additional dirt in as needed. Standard topsoil will work, but many suppliers sell special mixes for raised beds. You can also just shovel the dirt in as you build

the wall up. Estimate the amount of soil you need by measuring the inside width and height in feet. Soil is sold in cubic feet by the bag or cubic yards when bought in bulk. The rock wall doesn't need to be self-supporting if it's built into the soil. If the wall is closer to vertical, dig the trench wider and 5 to 6" deep and tamp in a few inches of crushed gravel (usually called Class 5). Make the wall thick enough to be solid and self-supporting, and wedge small rocks and chips in as needed to keep the stones locked in place

Pick out the most interesting stones in the pile as you work, and try to make them prominent. Mixing different sizes makes a denser, more varied wall.

HOW TO BUILD A SLOPING ROCK WALL

Mark out the site and dig a shallow trench for the rocks. If the area is weedy, or on a slope, or the rock wall will be very low, excavate enough so that the raised bed will have 12 to 18" of topsoil. If the soil is clay, replace it with equal parts loam, peat moss, and coarse sand.

Use the largest stones for the base, setting them in so they look partially buried, with the most weathered side exposed. Avoid even spacing or straight-looking rows, and vary sizes. Pack soil in, or, if you don't intend to have plants in the wall, place landscape fabric behind the rocks. Continue piling rocks around the area of the raised bed. Once the rocks are in place, cover the soil with mulch.

You can encourage a weathered, mossy look by "painting" the rocks with a handful of moss mixed in a blender with a cup of buttermilk or yogurt. This will give moss and lichen a good start.

After the soil has settled for a few days, begin planting the garden. Focus on plants native to your area. You can plant several sizes, from tiny alpine flowers to small shrubs and trees. Place plants in the crevices, allowing them to cascade over the rocks.

Add a birdbath and other decorations to your raised bed rock garden. You can add more colors during the warmer months by setting potted indoor plants among the rocks.

This raised bed framed by large stones and boulders looks like a natural rock outcropping, and blends in perfectly on the open, gently sloping yard. Use a heavy-duty dolly or rent a small front-end loader for this project—large boulders can weigh several hundred pounds.

HALF-LAP PLANTING BED

The half-lap is a traditional woodworking joint used to build everything from fine furniture to timber-frame barns. It creates a very strong connection and is more visually appealing than a standard butt joint or a simple overlap of the mating pieces. In this application, a raised bed benefits from the half-lap's strength, but it's the handcrafted look that makes this joint worth the extra trouble.

You can use any standard size of square-edged timber for this project: 4 x 4, 4 x 6, 6 x 6, etc. The smaller landscape timbers with rounded edges can also be used, but are much harder to work with. The trick to making half-lap joints is notching out exactly half of the thickness (or depth) from each mating piece so that the completed joint is equal to a whole timber. If you have a shop and a thickness planer, it's a good idea to first plane all your pieces to precisely the same size before setting up your tools for making identical notches in each piece. Timbers, especially the wet ones sold at home centers, often vary slightly in size, and many are slightly thicker at the centers because of uneven drying, and will rock slightly when placed on a flat surface. It's best to measure the timbers against each other and keep similar sizes together as you mark and cut the notches for each joint, and then keep them together as you construct the planting bed.

(continued next page)

If you have a few projects under your belt and want to try your hand at something a bit more challenging, this half-lap raised bed may be just the ticket for you.

- (Quantities are for a 3 ft. x 5 ft. bed)
- (6) 4 x 4" x 8-ft. cedar or pressure-treated
- (2) 2 x 6" x 8-ft. cedar or pressure-treated
- 3" deck screws or 16D galvanized nails (5 lb. box)
- 3" galvanized casing nails
- Wide wood chisel (1" minimum)
- Compactable gravel (optional)
- 6" spikes (24)
- Tape measure
- Speed square
- Circular saw
- Hammer or mallet
- 4-ft. level
- Drill
- Countersink bit

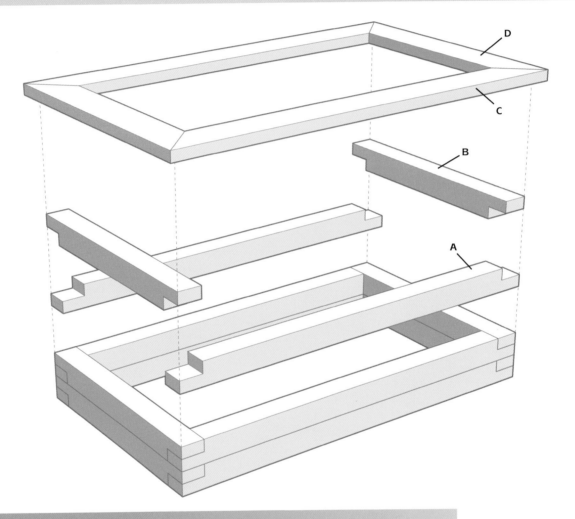

CUTTING LIST

KEY	PART	DIMENSION	PCS.	MATERIAL
A	Side	4 x 4 x 59"	6	Cedar or pressure-treated
B	End	4 x 4 x 35"	6	Cedar or pressure-treated
C	Side cap	2 x 6 x 62"	2	Cedar or pressure-treated
D	End cap	2 x 6 x 38"	2	Cedar or pressure-treated

HOW TO MAKE A HALF-LAP PLANTER

Cut the 4 x 4 stock to length to make your parts. You may find it faster to gang-cut two or three 4 x 4s at the same time, using a circular saw if the 4 x 4s are the exact same thickness. Simply clamp them together with their ends flush, make a cut with a circular saw along the cutting line, and then flip the stock over and finish cutting from the opposite side so the cuts line up. Make the cuts for the half-lap joints. Select pieces that are the same size, then put the flattest side (the side that rocks the least) of each board on a work surface facing down. Mark the 3½" shoulder cuts, arranging them so the best sides will face out when the project is assembled. Set the cutting depth of your circular saw to 1¾" and cut along the inside (3½" side) of the marked line. Then make a series of cuts parallel to this cut, spacing them about ¼" apart. These are called kerf cuts, and the point is to remove as much waste wood as you safely can. Be careful to keep the saw flat on the wood at the beginning and end of the cuts—it's easy to accidentally tip it.

Tip: You can also make these cuts on a sliding compound miter saw if it has a built-in depth stop. Or, get hold of a power miter saw (see above) with enough cutting capacity to get through a 4 x 4 in one pass.

Complete each notch by breaking out the waste pieces with a hammer or mallet. Clean up the bottom of the notch with a wood chisel, then test the half-lap joint with the adjoining timber and adjust as needed.

3 Form the half-lap joints. Lay out two long members on a flat surface with the notches facing up. Set a pair of shorter members—the ends—across the longer ones with their notches down. Test the fit and ensure that this base layer is square. Fasten each half-lap joint with a pair of screws or nails positioned diagonally over the notches, alternating the placement of the screws from level to level. Predrill if the wood starts to crack when you drive the screw in.

Add the next layer, keeping the sides of the raised bed flush and plumb. Drill pilot holes and drive a couple of 6" landscape spikes through the boards in each course and into the course below.

4 After the 4 x 4s are all assembled, you can leave the raised bed as is or add a 2 x 6 cap for a more finished appearance, and to make a comfortable place to sit. To create a cap with the 1½" overhang shown here, measure the outside of the frame and add 3". This will give you the length for the long edge of the 45° miter cut. Cut the four pieces, then set them in place and fiddle with them until the miters look tight. It may help to pin or screw a few of the outside corners together. Again, unless you've used a thickness planer, the construction grade wood will have slight variations and cupping that make a furniture-quality miter joint impossible, so just do the best you can and then sand the joints to even them out. You can also fiddle with the overhang if necessary—it will never be noticed.

This half-lap planting bed was made from round posts. It has an appealing appearance, but cutting the half-laps requires patience and skill.

■ Tip

Before filling your completed bed with soil, you can protect the timbers from premature rot by lining the insides of the walls with heavy (6-mil or thicker) plastic sheeting. Just make sure to line the walls only, not the bottom of the bed. Another option is to set the timbers atop a trench (underneath the timbers only) of compacted gravel to allow water to drain away, which will forestall rot and help keep the bed level over time. Also add a layer of newspaper over the ground before putting new soil in to smother any weeds and grasses.

RESOURCES

American Horticultural Society
You'll find information about plants, gardens, and more at this site.
www.ahs.org
(800) 777-7931

American Society of Landscape Architects (ASLA)
If you want to completely reimagine a large yard, you may want to turn
to a landscape architect. Find one at the ASLA website, along with other
information.
www.asla.org
(888) 999-ASLA

Association of Professional Landscape Designers (APLD)
Whether you just need a little assistance setting up a backyard
garden or want to completely redo a large yard, you can find member
professionals in your area by perusing the listings on the APLD's website.
www.apld.com
(717) 238-9780

Black & Decker
Turn to B&D for all the tools you'll need to create and maintain your
dream landscape.
www.blackanddecker.com

National Gardening Association
General information and resources related to gardening.
www.garden.org
(802) 863-5251

Greenland Gardener
Raised Garden Kits, page 152
www.greenlandgardener.com
877-586-2376

REFERENCE CHARTS

Drill Bit Guide

Twist Bit

Self-piloting

Spade Bit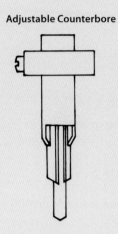

Adjustable Counterbore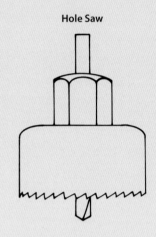

Hole Saw

Counterbore, Shank & Pilot Hole Diameters

Screw Size	Counterbore Diameter for Screw Head	Clearance Hole for Screw Shank	Pilot Hole Diameter	
			Hard Wood	Soft Wood
#1	.146 9/64	5/64	3/64	1/32
#2	1/4	3/32	3/64	1/32
#3	1/4	7/64	1/16	3/64
#4	1/4	1/8	1/16	3/64
#5	1/4	9/64	5/64	1/16
#6	5/16	5/32	3/32	5/64
#7	5/16	5/32	3/32	5/64
#8	3/8	11/64	1/8	3/32
#9	3/8	11/64	1/8	3/32
#10	3/8	3/16	1/8	7/64
#11	1/2	3/16	5/32	9/64
#12	1/2	7/32	9/64	1/8

Abrasive Paper Grits - (Aluminum Oxide)

Very Coarse	Coarse	Medium	Fine	Very Fine
12 - 36	40 - 60	80 - 120	150 - 180	220 - 600

Metric Conversions

To Convert:	To:	Multiply by:
Inches	Millimeters	25.4
Inches	Centimeters	2.54
Feet	Meters	0.305
Yards	Meters	0.914
Square inches	Square centimeters	6.45
Square feet	Square meters	0.093
Square yards	Square meters	0.836
Ounces	Milliliters	30.0
Pints (U.S.)	Liters	0.473 (Imp. 0.568)
Quarts (U.S.)	Liters	0.946 (Imp. 1.136)
Gallons (U.S.)	Liters	3.785 (Imp. 4.546)
Ounces	Grams	28.4
Pounds	Kilograms	0.454

To Convert:	To:	Multiply by:
Millimeters	Inches	0.039
Centimeters	Inches	0.394
Meters	Feet	3.28
Meters	Yards	1.09
Square centimeters	Square inches	0.155
Square meters	Square feet	10.8
Square meters	Square yards	1.2
Milliliters	Ounces	.033
Liters	Pints (U.S.)	2.114 (Imp. 1.76)
Liters	Quarts (U.S.)	1.057 (Imp. 0.88)
Liters	Gallons (U.S.)	0.264 (Imp. 0.22)
Grams	Ounces	0.035
Kilograms	Pounds	2.2

Converting Temperatures

Convert degrees Fahrenheit (F) to degrees Celsius (C) by following this simple formula: Subtract 32 from the Fahrenheit temperature reading. Then, multiply that number by 5/9. For example, 77°F - 32 = 45. 45 × 5/9 = 25°C.

To convert degrees Celsius to degrees Fahrenheit, multiply the Celsius temperature reading by 9/5. Then, add 32. For example, 25°C × 9/5 = 45. 45 + 32 = 77°F.

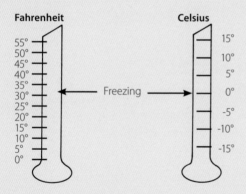

Metric Plywood Panels

Metric plywood panels are commonly available in two sizes: 1,200 mm × 2,400 mm and 1,220 mm × 2,400 mm, which is roughly equivalent to a 4 × 8-ft. sheet. Standard and Select sheathing panels come in standard thicknesses, while Sanded grade panels are available in special thicknesses.

Standard Sheathing Grade		Sanded Grade	
7.5 mm	(5/16 in.)	6 mm	(4/17 in.)
9.5 mm	(3/8 in.)	8 mm	(5/16 in.)
12.5 mm	(1/2 in.)	11 mm	(7/16 in.)
15.5 mm	(5/8 in.)	14 mm	(9/16 in.)
18.5 mm	(3/4 in.)	17 mm	(2/3 in.)
20.5 mm	(13/16 in.)	19 mm	(3/4 in.)
22.5 mm	(7/8 in.)	21 mm	(13/16 in.)
25.5 mm	(1 in.)	24 mm	(15/16 in.)

Lumber Dimensions

Nominal - U.S.	Actual - U.S. (in inches)	Metric
1 × 2	3/4 × 1 1/2	19 × 38 mm
1 × 3	3/4 × 2 1/2	19 × 64 mm
1 × 4	3/4 × 3 1/2	19 × 89 mm
1 × 5	3/4 × 4 1/2	19 × 114 mm
1 × 6	3/4 × 5 1/2	19 × 140 mm
1 × 7	3/4 × 6 1/4	19 × 159 mm
1 × 8	3/4 × 7 1/4	19 × 184 mm
1 × 10	3/4 × 9 1/4	19 × 235 mm
1 × 12	3/4 × 11 1/4	19 × 286 mm
1 1/4 × 4	1 × 3 1/2	25 × 89 mm
1 1/4 × 6	1 × 5 1/2	25 × 140 mm
1 1/4 × 8	1 × 7 1/4	25 × 184 mm
1 1/4 × 10	1 × 9 1/4	25 × 235 mm
1 1/4 × 12	1 × 11 1/4	25 × 286 mm
1 1/2 × 4	1 1/4 × 3 1/2	32 × 89 mm
1 1/2 × 6	1 1/4 × 5 1/2	32 × 140 mm
1 1/2 × 8	1 1/4 × 7 1/4	32 × 184 mm
1 1/2 × 10	1 1/4 × 9 1/4	32 × 235 mm
1 1/2 × 12	1 1/4 × 11 1/4	32 × 286 mm
2 × 4	1 1/2 × 3 1/2	38 × 89 mm
2 × 6	1 1/2 × 5 1/2	38 × 140 mm
2 × 8	1 1/2 × 7 1/4	38 × 184 mm
2 × 10	1 1/2 × 9 1/4	38 × 235 mm
2 × 12	1 1/2 × 11 1/4	38 × 286 mm
3 × 6	2 1/2 × 5 1/2	64 × 140 mm
4 × 4	3 1/2 × 3 1/2	89 × 89 mm
4 × 6	3 1/2 × 5 1/2	89 × 140 mm

Liquid Measurement Equivalents

1 Pint	= 16 Fluid Ounces	= 2 Cups
1 Quart	= 32 Fluid Ounces	= 2 Pints
1 Gallon	= 128 Fluid Ounces	= 4 Quarts

INDEX